# The Faith and Friendships of Teenage Boys

# THE FAITH AND FRIENDSHIPS OF TEENAGE BOYS

*Robert C. Dykstra, Allan Hugh Cole Jr., and Donald Capps*

WESTMINSTER JOHN KNOX PRESS
LOUISVILLE · KENTUCKY

*First edition*
Published by Westminster John Knox Press
Louisville, Kentucky

12 13 14 15 16 17 18 19 20 21—10 9 8 7 6 5 4 3 2 1

*Book design by Sharon Adams*
*Cover design by designpointinc.com*

**Library of Congress Cataloging-in-Publication Data**

Dykstra, Robert C., 1956–
    The faith and friendships of teenage boys / Robert C. Dykstra, Allan Hugh Cole, Jr., and Donald Capps. — 1st ed.
        p. cm.
    Includes bibliographical references (p.      ) and index.
    ISBN 978-0-664-23340-2 (alk. paper)
    1. Teenage boys—Religious life. 2. Christian teenagers—Religious life. 3. Friendship—Religious aspects—Christianity. I. Cole, Allan Hugh. II. Capps, Donald. III. Title.
    BV4541.3.D95 2012
    248.8'32—dc23

                                                                    2012010947

Most Westminster John Knox Press books are available at special quantity discounts when purchased in bulk by corporations, organizations, and special-interest groups. For more information, please e-mail SpecialSales@wjkbooks.com.

To our friends
Anthony Genosa and Robert Drago
and
Jonathan Eastman

# Contents

# Acknowledgments

We appreciate the opportunity to work with Westminster John Knox Press on a second book about the experiences and needs of adolescent boys. The leadership of president Marc Lewis, the vision of David Dobson and the editorial staff, the efficiency and grace of Julie Tonini and the production staff, the strategy of Tom Parmenter and the marketing group, along with Emily Kiefer's energy and creativity as publicist, make us both proud and grateful to work with such a fine press. We also want to thank Frances Purifoy for her work as copyeditor.

We began work on this book with Jon L. Berquist, our longtime friend and editor at WJK, who urged us to write a "follow-up" to our first book on boys, *Losers, Loners, and Rebels: The Spiritual Struggles of Boys* (Louisville, KY: Westminster John Knox Press, 2007), and who helped us think more clearly about how we would approach this current book and about what our focus would be. Jon's wisdom and guidance proved invaluable as we proceeded. As the book neared completion, we began working with a new editor, Jana Riess, whose close reading of the manuscript and whose perceptive insights have helped us improve the book in numerous ways. We are grateful for both Jon's and Jana's interest in and dedication to the lives of young people and for helping us speak more clearly and honestly to those who love and care for adolescent boys.

Allan Cole is grateful for the editorial and other supportive assistance provided by Alison Riemersma, administrative assistant to the office of the academic dean at Austin Seminary. We also appreciate the efforts of Katie Frederick, a student at Austin Seminary, who prepared the book's index with precision and speed.

Finally, we are grateful to those who devote their lives, whether personally, vocationally, or both, to nurturing and celebrating the lives of boys, their faith, and their friendships.

# Introduction

Martin, a seventeen-year-old boy, speaks to a link between friendship and faith for adolescent boys:

> It's so important to have people you can talk to about serious things. My immediate friends, we definitely have deep conversations about religion, things that are going on, and creative ideas that we have. And that's essential for us. . . . For some reason, I feel like I'm at a point in my life right now where I don't know what to think about religion. As soon as I came out of the womb I was Christian, because my parents were Christian. I've gone to a Methodist church all my life. At a young age you go to church because it's just that's the way things are, but now I'm at an age where I'm questioning religion and the faith I've always grown up with. I don't really have any problems with the church, but that's the only thing I've been exposed to and I think there's something more. I don't think the Bible is the only place where truth is. I think I should try to look into other things and not be too closed-minded. Just because I grew up with these certain beliefs and my parents are that way doesn't mean I should stay that way. (Pollack 2000, 98–99)

This book is largely about friendships among adolescent boys, especially links between their friendships and their faith. It also seeks to offer a response to Martin and to other boys who have an interest in deeper relationships, in deeper life questions and religious questions, and who seek to discern more about how friendship and faith may be related.

Churches place a great deal of emphasis on the spiritual formation of adolescents. Many churches have a full-time youth minister or director who concentrates on this age group, and churches are often evaluated on the basis of whether or not they have a vital youth group. Why this emphasis on boys and girls in this age bracket?

There are good historical reasons for this emphasis. The early church developed the concept of the catechumen, a person who would receive instruction in the Christian faith and on successful completion of this instruction would be admitted to membership in the church. The catechumen could be virtually any age, for adults were expected to be catechumens before they were admitted to the faith. But children reared by Christian parents would normally enter the catechumen instruction process in their middle teens. Over the centuries, many Christian denominations have followed this tradition and have developed instructional materials for use by pastors or other adults who have the responsibility of certifying a young person for full membership in the church. These instructional materials are usually designed for young persons in their adolescent years.

There are also good psychological reasons for this emphasis on adolescents. In his book *The Individual and His Religion*, Gordon W. Allport (1950), then a well-known Harvard professor of psychology and active member of the Episcopal Church, noted,

> Usually it is not until the stress of puberty that serious reverses occur in the evolution of the religious sentiment. At this period of development the youth is compelled to transform his religious attitudes—indeed all his attitudes—from second-hand fittings to first-hand fittings of his personality. He can no longer let his parents do his thinking for him. Although in some cases the transition is fluent and imperceptible, more often there is a period of rebellion. (32)

Allport cites various studies showing that approximately two-thirds of all adolescents react against parental and cultural teaching. Approximately half of the rebellions come before the age of sixteen, and half later. Rebellion takes many forms:

> Sometimes the youth simply shifts his allegiance to a religious institution different from his parents'. Or he may reach a satisfying rationalism from which religious considerations are forever after eliminated. Sometimes, when the first shadows of doubt appear, he gives up the whole problem and drifts into the style of life, said to be characteristic of modern youth, of opportunism and hedonism. Occasionally the storm arises not because of intellectual doubts, but because of a gnawing sense of guilt and shame, due perhaps to sexual conflicts. (33)

Allport cites other studies showing that three forms of religious awakening are commonly experienced. One is the *definite crisis* or conversion experience.

Another is an *emotional stimulus* type of awakening in which the upheaval is slight or absent, but the teenager is able to designate some single event that served as the effective stimulus to his religious reorientation. The third is a *gradual awakening*, with no specifiable occasion being decisive. The studies indicate that about 70 percent of the religious awakenings are of the third type, and the remaining 30 percent are almost equally divided between the other two.

These studies also show that in cases with a marked turn or vivid experience there are usually consequences of a lasting, and often permanent, order. At the same time, the major significance of the *definite crisis* or *emotional stimulus* lies in the hunger it arouses and in the charting of a direction of search for appeasing this hunger. Almost always the adolescent who has experienced a vividly religious state of mind seeks throughout his life to recapture its inspiration. Thus the religious or spiritual awakenings of adolescents are the beginning, not the conclusion, of a search or quest. Also, as time goes on, the religious sentiment overlaps and blends with other sentiments. For example, adolescents who fall in love find that the exalted selflessness of this state is not unlike the mystical experience they may have in their religious moments. Or romantic ideals of accomplishment may occupy their minds, and their ambitions may merge with a religious longing to embrace the whole universe.

On the other hand, adolescence is the time when one is expected, if not by family members then at least by one's contemporaries, to scrutinize all established ways of looking at things. This scrutiny typically takes the form of critiques of the school and church that one attends, the home in which one lives, and the social system that one learns about in school and in which one participates. Rejection of these established institutions is one way of stepping forth as an independent adult in a culture where one is expected to outstrip one's parents in occupational, social, and educational accomplishments (32–36).

Allport's concluding chapter on the nature of faith ends with a brief section titled "The Solitary Way" in which he notes that from its early beginnings to the end of the road the religious or spiritual quest of the individual is a solitary one: "Though he is socially interdependent with others in a thousand ways, yet no one else is able to provide him with the faith he evolves, nor prescribe for him his pact with the cosmos" (141–42). This statement, which appears on the concluding page of Allport's book, is the starting point for our own book. We believe that it is true—that the faith each one of us evolves is necessarily our own and not provided by anyone else. We also believe, however, that certain individuals are more likely than others to support us in this personal quest, and precisely because they are supportive, we call them *friends*. A friend may also play other social roles in our lives. A parent or pastor or teacher can be a friend. But, as Allport has pointed out, our contemporaries are the most likely to expect us to scrutinize critically all established ways of looking at things. Thus the persons who are most likely to support an adolescent boy in his personal religious or spiritual quest are other adolescents.

Another inspiration for this book is Ralph Waldo Emerson, the minister-turned-writer who had an enormous influence on younger persons in his day who were struggling against the established ways of looking at things. He is best known for his essay "Self-Reliance" (Emerson 1983, 257–82), in which he encourages his readers to become autonomous, independent individuals and not "capitulate to badges and names, to large societies and dead institutions" (262). The key themes in his appeal for personal autonomy are (1) the spontaneous freedom exhibited by children—or, as he more colorfully puts it, "the nonchalance of boys who are sure of a dinner" (261)—especially in not calculating the consequences of one's actions but in cutting through appearances to the truth; (2) the refusal to be a slave to one's past, especially that for which one became known or recognized; (3) resistance to the demands for social conformity and unquestioning compliance; and (4) the courage to trust oneself—one's own perceptions, one's judgments, and the testimony of one's own experience. Emerson takes for granted that the religious or spiritual quest is a personal one and that although we are socially interdependent with others in a thousand ways, no one is able to provide us with the faith that we evolve.

But Emerson also wrote an essay titled "Friendship" (1983, 341–54) that bids us to think of how many persons we meet in the street or sit beside in church with whom, though we might be silent, we warmly rejoice to be. Then he focuses on the persons, fewer in number, whom we count as personal friends. He says that he awoke this very morning "with devout thanksgiving for my friends, the old and the new" (342). He dares to call God "the Beautiful" because God is revealed in gifts like these, and adds that all of his friends have come to him as though unsought for "the great God gave them to me" (342–43). He says that he does not want "to treat friendships daintily, but with roughest courage" for "when they are real, they are not glass threads or frostwork but the solidest thing we know" (346). Friendship, in his view, has two basic elements. One is *truth*: "A friend is a person with whom I may be sincere" (347). The other is *tenderness*: "When a man becomes dear to me, I have touched the goal of fortune" (348). Friendship is also the most solid thing we know: "It is for aid and comfort through all the relations and passages of life and death. It is fit for serene days, and graceful gifts, and country rambles, but also for rough roads and hard fare, shipwreck, poverty, and persecution" (348–49). Friends also respect their differences, for friendship is "an alliance of two large, formidable natures, mutually beheld, mutually feared, before yet they recognize the deep identity which beneath these disparities unites them" (350). He notes that if one's offer of friendship is not returned, this is no disgrace, for, in fact, "thou art enlarged by thy own shining." In the final analysis, however, "the essence of friendship is entireness, a total magnanimity and trust" (354).

Emerson wrote these words about friendship 170 years ago, but they are as relevant today as they were then. The ways that friendships are formed, expressed, and maintained reflect the social contexts in which they occur, but the basic elements of friendship haven't changed, for friendships that lack either truth or tenderness do not endure. What is equally important for our purposes here is Emerson's claim that friendship is an alliance in which two persons maintain their own distinct identities and yet share a deep identity that unites them. So we do not dispute—in fact, we embrace and affirm—Allport's view that the religious or spiritual quest is a solitary one, but we also believe that its solitariness is mitigated when one has a friend for a traveling companion. And is it not the case for others, as it was for Emerson, that such friendships are themselves a gift from God?

As we reflected on the focus of this book, our thoughts were naturally drawn to the biblical story of the friendship between David and Jonathan. David and Jonathan met the day that David slew Goliath. King Saul, Jonathan's father, had summoned David to him so that he could find out whose son David was. When David replied that he was the son of Jesse of Bethlehem, "the soul of Jonathan was bound to the soul of David, and Jonathan loved him as his own soul" (1 Sam. 18:1). Jonathan also made a covenant with David and gave him his robe, armor, sword, and belt, and Saul invited David to live with him and his family. David was successful in whatever battles Saul sent him out to wage, but his successes made Saul envious of him, and he instructed Jonathan and all his servants to kill David. Jonathan, however, informed David of Saul's instructions, helped him to hide, and also persuaded his father to withdraw his order. But when David returned to live in Saul's home, Saul again threatened him, and David fled. Jonathan reassured David that he would continue to inform him of his father's intentions and urged David, in return, not to cut off his loyalty to him and his family. He made David swear again his love for him because Jonathan "loved him as he loved his own life" (1 Sam. 20:17).

Saul, however, became angry with Jonathan, telling him that as long as David lived, Jonathan would not succeed his father as the king. David was simply too popular with the people. So Saul again vowed that he would kill David. Jonathan rose from the table in great anger because his father had disgraced him, and the next day he sought out the place where David was hiding. They kissed one another and wept until David was eventually able to compose himself. Jonathan was now convinced that his father would do everything he could to lay his hands on David to kill him. All Jonathan could do for his friend was to reassure him that he seriously doubted that his father would be able to find David. He went out once again to see David, but this appears to have been their last meeting together. Although Saul continued to pursue David, he was unsuccessful in his efforts. In fact, David had a chance to kill Saul when he encountered the king asleep and unprotected in a cave, but he chose not to do so. He could not bring himself to kill the father of his best friend. Saul and his sons eventually met their death when the Philistines overtook them. The Philistines slew Jonathan and his two brothers, and Saul, badly wounded, fell upon his own sword and died.

When David learned of what had happened, he mourned the deaths of Saul and Jonathan, declaring his love for both of them. But his deepest love was reserved for Jonathan. He spoke these words:

> I am distressed for you, my brother Jonathan;
> greatly beloved you were to me;
> your love to me was wonderful,
> passing the love of women.
>                                    (2 Sam. 1:26)

Theirs had been a friendship based on truth and tenderness. It was a gift from God. Although one was the son of a shepherd and the other was the son of a king, there was a deep identity between them. Theirs was a faithful friendship, a close friendship, and for Jonathan especially but also for David, a subversive friendship.

This book, then, reflects our conviction that even as David spoke to his friend Jonathan as if he were still alive, so is the very spirit of their friendship alive with us today. We believe it is found among adolescent boys and plays a central role in their struggle to transform their religious attitudes—indeed all their attitudes—from secondhand fittings to firsthand fittings as they seek to develop a faith of their own. Furthermore, we believe that friendship is implicated in the hunger that the religious awakening of teenagers arouses and in the charting of a direction of search for appeasing this hunger. In other words, friendship is more than a resource on which an adolescent boy may draw in order to help him make his way forward. It is also integral to how a boy comes to understand the destination itself. If friendship is based on truth and tenderness, it makes perfect sense to think of it as an expression of faith. Indeed, boys' friendships often *are* their faith. This was certainly true of the friendship of David and Jonathan.

The chapters that we have written here reflect this way of viewing friendship, personal faith, and their profoundly related roles in the spiritual journeys of adolescent boys. The first and second chapters (by Allan Cole) on faithful friendships, the third and fourth chapters (by Robert Dykstra) on subversive friendships, and the fifth chapter (by Donald Capps) on close friendships present complementary understandings of how adolescent boys' personal friendships and personal faith together inspire their spiritual journeys. Thus, these chapters are reflections on the adolescent boy's attempt, as Allport puts it, "to enlarge and to complete his own personality by finding the supreme context in which he rightly belongs" (142).

More specifically, chapter 1 on faithful friendships draws on the story of a boyhood friend's struggle with baseball to explore roles that friendships play in forming a boy's identity. Such friendships foster the boy's ability to believe in himself, in others, in worthy ideals, and in God. In these ways, friendships shape his spiritual life. Chapter 2 on friendship as boyhood spirituality shows how friendships serve a boy by providing a context for him to develop and maintain particular psychospiritual strengths. These strengths sustain him when he faces various struggles, especially ones that relate to his sense of failure to meet expectations placed on him by social norms of boyhood and manhood.

Chapter 3 on subversive friendships considers certain unrelenting psychosocial and spiritual pressures that increasingly burden boys' same-sex friendships as they approach adulthood. While to a certain extent such pressures are inevitable given the complexities of human sexuality, they are exacerbated both by church teachings that privilege the spiritual over the physical and by cultural codes that too narrowly circumscribe the acceptable range of masculine conduct and desire. As a result, friendships with other boys come to seem dangerous or nearly impossible for adolescent boys, leading one pastoral theologian to suggest that their "fear of intimate male friendships is one of the most critical forms of oppression under which they live" (Culbertson 1996, 174). Chapter 4 suggests constructive ways in which those who care for adolescent boys, including Christian youth leaders as well as boys themselves in their friendships with one another, can better understand and enhance their ability to navigate the tensions discussed in chapter 3. These strategies emphasize that while there may be no ultimate cure for the complexities boys experience in their friendships with other boys, their caregivers and friends can nonetheless learn to recognize and honor the unique, earthy, and often overlooked means by which boys actually can and do express intimacy and faith.

Chapter 5 focuses on close friendships that fit Emerson's understanding of friendship as tender and truthful. It relates several contemporary boys' accounts of their close friendships with other boys in William S. Pollack's (2000) *Real Boys' Voices*, then focuses on the close friendship that began to form between Capps, the author of this chapter, and the adolescent boy who continues to live inside of him. This friendship may well be prototypical of

Emerson's suggestion that a friendship is a relationship between two individuals who, despite their significant disparities, share a deep identity that unites them as one. This chapter also supports Allport's (1950) claim about the solitary nature of an individual's religious quest but suggests that one may be solitary but not necessarily alone. Capps illustrates this point with a short story that he wrote in his junior year of high school that provides the basis for reflections on the continuing presence of the adolescent boy in the ongoing religious quest of the older man and with a poem written in his senior year on the story in the Gospel of Luke (24:13–35) about the two men who were heading toward a village named Emmaus. He imagines that the travelers are himself as the adolescent boy and the old man and that they are joined and connected together—by the stranger whose own identity is revealed to them. The chapter concludes with discussion of a poem on David and Jonathan by John Henry Newman that concerns the termination of close friendships and the reasons for it.

We should note that we have focused throughout this book on adolescent boys' friendships with other adolescent boys. We are aware, of course, that these are years in which boys often experience friendships with girls, some of which have sexual overtones (and undertones as well) and others of which do not. We believe that the same basic elements of friendship—of truth and tenderness—apply here as well. But we have chosen to focus on male friendships because we wanted to address the fact that the claim that we are making here—that friendships are an expression of faith—receives less support in Christian writings and practice when the friendships involve two boys or two men; when, as David says of his friendship with Jonathan, "Your love to me was wonderful, passing the love of women." We identify some of the reasons for the church's deeply held suspicions of same-sex male friendships and explore the effects of these suspicions on adolescent boys, especially the fact that they make the boy's quest for friendship and for faith more solitary than it was ever intended to be.

Finally, this is our second book on adolescent boys. The first was titled *Losers, Loners, and Rebels: The Spiritual Struggles of Boys* (Dykstra, Cole, and Capps 2007). It focused especially on boys in their early adolescence, which is typically defined as the years between eleven and fourteen. We discovered, however, both in the writing of the first book and in conversations with its readers, that the identities of losers, loners, and rebels are not restricted to the early adolescent years. In fact, many boys do not identify with one or another of these self-images until their later adolescence, typically defined as the years between fourteen and eighteen. Survivors of the shootings that occurred at Columbine High School in Littleton, Colorado, in 1999, killing twelve students and injuring many others, referred to the boys who did the shooting as "losers" (Sandage 2005, 275). They were seventeen and eighteen years old.

The following chapters will provide ample evidence of the relevance of the three images of the loser, the loner, and the rebel to later adolescence, which is our primary focus in this book. But this book presents a fourth way in which all adolescent boys (younger and older) may identify themselves: as *friends*. This does not mean, of course, that the fourth self-identification is necessarily a separate category. After all, the two "losers" who shot and killed twelve of their fellow students and injured many others were also friends. More important, we contended in the earlier book that *loser*, *loner*, and *rebel* are not only negative terms, for there is a connection between the *loser* and self-awareness, the *loner* and self-transcendence, and the *rebel* and self-sufficiency, qualities that we suggested may be viewed as spiritual strengths. Conversely, as we discussed in our earlier book and maintain in this book as well, friendships among boys are not always models of truth and tenderness.[1] So we should avoid thinking of the loser, loner, and rebel in purely negative terms and of friends in purely positive terms.

On the other hand, there is something about the very word *friend* that is inspiring in a way that the others are not. This inspiring quality may be traced to the friendship of David and Jonathan, a friendship that Jesus may well have had in mind when he said to the men who had accompanied him on his own spiritual journey, " 'I do not call you servants any longer, because the servant does not know what the master is doing; but I have called you friends, because I have made known to you everything that I have heard from my Father' " (John 15:15). As we have seen, Jonathan disclosed to his friend David what he had heard from his father Saul. Of course, the intentions of the two fathers in these cases were very different, but the point is that friends share what they know with one another.

If Jesus had made this affirmative declaration in the company of adolescent boys today, he could have said that he does not call them "losers," "loners," and "rebels"—not, however, because these labels are untrue but because even as he did not hesitate to befriend losers, loners, and rebels then, he does not hesitate to befriend them today. In his well-known poem (later set to music by Charles C. Converse) "What a Friend We Have in Jesus," Joseph Scriven asks, "Can we find a friend so faithful, who will all our sorrows share?"[2] The answer, of course, is no. But this doesn't mean that we can't awake in the morning with devout thanksgiving for our friends or dare to call God "the Beautiful" because God is revealed to us in such gifts as these.

# PART I

# Faithful Friendships

ALLAN HUGH COLE JR.

# 1

# Faithful Friendships

Ken was on my seventh-grade baseball team. He was awful at baseball. Tall and skinny, he lacked muscular coordination. Walking on his tiptoes, he bounced along with the agility of a young colt learning to walk. Like a colt, sometimes he appeared on the verge of falling flat on his face.

Even with this awkwardness, Ken was a friendly kid. Somewhat shy, he never sought attention; but he was social enough. Many of us on the baseball team felt sorry for him due to his lack of athleticism, but we genuinely liked him and fully included him in team life. He was viewed as being as much a part of the team as anyone else. Looking back, I wonder if his awkwardness with baseball garnered our empathy because it reminded us of our own awkwardness in those years, whether with regard to sports, school, girls, parents—or *life*.

Team life included not only baseball practice and games but also trips to get hamburgers and ice cream after games and subsequent gatherings at various boys' homes. We boys appreciated the friendships we formed that season. We also appreciated Ken's obvious efforts to improve at baseball. He maintained a faithful presence at practices and at games. He worked hard to enhance his skills, and his efforts made the rest of us work harder too. Perhaps a part of Ken believed that if he just kept at it and practiced enough he'd reach some level of acceptable performance in baseball, though I'm not sure what acceptable would have meant to him.

Despite his dutiful presence at practice and his efforts to improve, Ken got little time on the field during games. The only reason he was put into a game at all was that the youth baseball league required coaches to play each boy at least two innings in every game. This meant that when Ken got into a game, it

3

was never before the seventh inning. He was placed in right field, where there was the least chance of his having a ball hit to him and dropping it. He was also inserted in the bottom of the batting order because as bad as he was in the field, he was worse at batting. He *always* struck out, usually without making contact with any ball thrown to him. More times than not, a ball pitched to him reached the catcher's mitt before Ken swung his bat. It was as if he could swing only after hearing the pop of leather.

I remember feeling deep pain over seeing Ken struggle, and also a predictable dread when I saw him trot onto the field. I think my teammates and all of our parents felt this dread too. It still pains me to imagine what Ken must have felt. Practice after practice, game after game, I sensed that he longed to find any measure of success, *something* to affirm him in his efforts. We boys tried to affirm him—after all, he was our friend—as did the coaches, his parents, and other parents who watched. We said things like "Keep your head up," "You'll get 'em next time," and "Good effort, Ken." But despite our encouragements, success and a corresponding possibility for *self*-affirmation seemed always at bay. Ken would concentrate, clench his teeth, and let out a grunt when he swung the bat. Playing right field, he made sure to use two hands when trying to catch a ball hit his way—a fundamentally sound way to play the game. But despite his commitment to work on the fundamentals of baseball, he continued to fail.

I also got the sense that although he worked very hard to improve his game, Ken really didn't want to play baseball, at least not in the way that others of us did. His father wanted him to play. This was clear. In fact, often after Ken struck out, he'd immediately glance into the stands as if to say, "I'm sorry" to his Dad—a gaze of both shame and yearning that I can still picture. But I never got the sense that Ken was putting himself through the struggles that came with baseball season because *he* loved the game and wanted to play it, though I do think that he valued the friendships he formed through baseball. I have also wondered whether he stuck with baseball not merely because his father wanted him to play but because the pleasure of sharing friendships with teammates exceeded the pain of being inept at baseball.

As the season continued, Ken's frustration level wore on him. He began to show it in his behavior. Routinely slamming the end of the bat to the ground when he struck out at the plate, he'd turn it in the dirt like a corkscrew. It was almost as if he thought that he could make the bat disappear if he turned it hard enough and perhaps make himself disappear too. At some point he'd start kicking the dirt as he walked back to the dugout, his head held low and shaking firmly back and forth as if to say, "No. No. No." Eventually, he would say at an audible level things like "I can't do anything right," "I suck," and, on one occasion, "I hate this fucking game."

Near the end of the season, after striking out the umpteenth time and verbally accosting himself as he walked back to the dugout, Ken could not hold
back his tears any longer. Laying his bat down, he walked briskly to the far
end of the bench, placed his moist face in his dirty, slender, boyish hands, and
wept. As he tried desperately to stop crying, his body shook with what must
have seemed to him like a lifetime of athletic failures.

One might assume that such an emotional release would prove helpful to
Ken, that crying would serve as a cathartic experience that helped uncork
what had been bottled so deep within him. In the right setting and circumstances, perhaps this assumption would prove correct. But in this case it was
different. In Ken's eyes, his crying only added insult to injury. He had learned
early in life that "real boys" not only were "studs" on the ball field but also
didn't cry. Like many boys, he believed that crying is for sissies and wimps—
for *girls*. Therefore, Ken's tearful episode, which happened of all places on
the quintessential American boy stage—a baseball field in front of numerous other boys on a summer's day—should have tapped out whatever self-
confidence, pride, or courage he still possessed.

I wish that I could remember more clearly how the coaches and Ken's parents responded to him that day, especially his father, but I don't. I do remember, however, that no one sought to console him, including me. I wanted to
console him, and I believe that others did too. But I think we boys understood
that doing so may have helped *us* feel better, but it would only further Ken's
pain. If there is anything worse for a boy than crying in front of one's male
friends, it's having one of those friends take note of it and offer consolation.
Teddy, a sixteen-year-old boy from the Midwest, speaks to why this would
have been so, not only for Ken but for most any boy in his situation:

> I don't cry in front of people, but I'll do it sometimes when I'm in my
> own room or talking to one of my good friends on the phone. But
> not in front of guys. It comes off as physically weak. You just don't
> amount to much as a guy if you cry in front of others. When I get
> upset about things, usually I just go to my room and isolate myself.
> I feel like I can't talk to my parents about it, and I can't talk to my
> brother about it. My parents would think something is wrong, like I
> am going to kill myself or something. And my brother, I can't really
> go crying to him because he's a guy, and the whole wimp thing comes
> into play again. (Pollack 2000, 42)

I suspect, in Ken's perception at least, that if there were any doubts about
his not being "all boy," he erased those doubts with the first wipe of his wet
eyes on the baseball field. The sanctuary of his own room beyond reach, he
settled for the lonely yet public humiliation of the end of the bench, a place
not of sanctuary but of isolation, and a place that he knew all too well.

I did not expect to see Ken on the field again following this tearful incident. I assumed that after feeling so humiliated, he would decline returning to the field, remain on the bench for the rest of the game, leave the dugout as inconspicuously as possible, and then quietly quit the team. And who would blame him if he did? Honestly, a part of me wanted him to quit—wanted to quit *for* him—so that he would be put out of his misery and the rest of us would be too. Our own misery was tied to seeing him struggle and feeling unable to help. But after a few moments, Ken retrieved his hat and glove, stood up, gave his dirt-streaked face one last, long wipe with his forearm and the back of his hand, and trotted out to his place in right field, where he completed the inning and finished the game without any additional failures.

Ken did not join the rest of us for a burger and ice cream after the game, and although we gently encouraged him to come with us, we understood why he declined. But Ken showed up at both practices that next week. He also made it to the game the following Saturday morning.

I remember admiring his courage even more than I had before. I also remember thinking that I would not have been so persistent or courageous myself. Part of the incongruity of my experiences with Ken is that, on the one hand, I felt sorry for him, but on the other hand, I admired him. I remember thinking that, in a strange way, he was actually a team leader, one who led by example in ways that I had only begun to recognize. He stunk at baseball, and when he got on the field, everyone feared not only that he would embarrass himself but that he'd make an error that would lose a close game. We were competitive boys who wanted to win, after all. But I think I was aware, even at a relatively young age, of my uncertainty about whether I or other boys on that team would have been able or willing to keep "stepping up to the plate" as he did. Ken's courage and perseverance earned our respect, even as his other personal qualities garnered our friendship.

## LIFE LESSONS

Commencing to write these chapters, I thought of Ken and of what he taught me about courage and perseverance. I also pondered what he taught me about friendships among adolescent boys. All of the lessons linked with him presented themselves in one baseball season when I was twelve years old. In fact, because we lived a great distance apart and I played the following season in a different town and baseball league, I never saw Ken again after we were teammates that one year. But I believe that these lessons and, more significant, my friendship with Ken, prepared me for more meaningful subsequent friendships in high school and beyond, in years marked by various kinds of ineptitude and awkwardness not unlike Ken's struggles with baseball.

I also believe that Ken's story can still teach us about boys and men. This book is for those who want to know boys and men better, and who in knowing them better desire to have stronger relationships with them. This book is also for men who want to know themselves more deeply, and who in doing so hope to form stronger relationships with others, as fathers, sons, husbands, partners, friends, brothers, and colleagues—as *men*. Ken's story and the friendships linked with it help us with these types of knowledge.

In this chapter and the next, I explore roles that friendships may play in a boy's life. Specifically, I consider how friendships affect a boy's identity formation; how friendships expand his capacities for belief (in himself, in others, in worthy ideals, and in God); and how friendships affect his spiritual life. I then suggest that friendships serve a boy by providing a context for developing and maintaining psychospiritual strengths, the kinds of nascent strengths I believe Ken possessed and drew on to sustain him amid all the disappointments of baseball and the strengths that we boys recognized and admired. Friendships encourage and support these psychospiritual strengths by helping a boy cultivate trust and trustworthiness and by helping him resist pressures to overcomply with social and familial expectations. In these ways, friendships relate to his budding identity and capacities for believing in himself, in others, and in God.

## DEFINING TERMS

Let me specify what I mean when using the terms *belief* and *spiritual life*. By *belief* I mean a "willingness to act" (James 1992b, 458) out of fidelity to an object of trust, and to do so because this object proves worthy of devotion by remaining true to its nature *and* true to the one devoted to it. I thus use the terms *belief in* and *faith in* synonymously. To believe in someone or something means to have faith in that person or thing, and vice versa.

By *spiritual life* I mean a life marked by qualities of trust, mutuality, and a benevolent self-image that offer a boy a sense of living amid a "hallowed presence"—that is, his sense of the presence of the Divine and its good intentions toward him *as a boy*. Furthermore, borrowing a concept from the psychologist Erik H. Erikson, a spiritual life also involves a person having a sense of "at-homeness" in the world. This at-homeness issues from and feeds back into a boy's confidence that who he is and the places that he occupies in the world remain "more or less in synch" with the rest of life (Cole 2008, 160–61). In other words, one fits in appropriately enough with the larger world, its workings, its norms, and its people.

Friendships provide boys with a measure of at-homeness, even in the midst of alienating experiences, in ways that I will detail. At-homeness includes feeling secure in the presence of sacred and divine things but also amid the more mundane settings of life, such as boyhood friends and baseball fields. This sense of at-homeness fosters a spiritual life by enhancing a person's capacities for trust and hope—including trust in others, trust in oneself, and, for those more spiritually inclined, trust in God.

From these understandings of belief (faith) and the spiritual life I make two principal claims. First, the identity formation of an older adolescent boy (ages fourteen to eighteen) depends on *and* further informs his capacity for belief in others (including God), in himself, and in worthy ideals (such as friendship). Second, a boy's friendships provide a context for developing his identity and faith because friendships foster trust and trustworthiness and because friendships have the potential for helping to mitigate the pressures that many boys feel to meet social expectations of boyhood. For boys more spiritually inclined, trusting and supportive friendships may also foster deeper trust in God and related spiritual matters. We find evidence for the power of friendships to foster spiritual growth among adolescents in church youth groups and parachurch organizations, where strong interpersonal bonds foster interest in and openness to things spiritual. Friendship thus holds the status of a psychospiritual strength for later adolescent boys. In the next chapter I will note how friendships may help a boy maintain psychological and spiritual well-being in adolescence and beyond as I return to Ken's story.

## AN INTROSPECTIVE APPROACH

An old saying holds that "the boy is father to the man." While this is something of an exaggeration, there can be little doubt that boys can teach men not only about boyhood but also about manhood. Grown men learn from boys by paying closer attention to them, by speaking with them about their experiences, and by seeking deeper emotional connections with them, all of which foster better understandings of life as *boys* experience it. A better understanding involves a deeper awareness of how boys view themselves, especially as compared with their perceptions of how others view them, and includes what boys appreciate, desire, and hope for; where they find meaning; and also the kinds of struggles they face. Engaging boys and learning about their experiences also serve to dispel powerful and often inaccurate myths about boyhood that inform societal norms for boys and influence how adults view and treat them. Greater insight into all of these matters of boyhood helps men relate to boys with more authenticity, intimacy, appreciation, and concern.

Learning from boys also helps men learn about themselves. This learning occurs as their experiences with boys invite men to ponder and revisit their own boyhoods, which we three have done and continue to do. Taking a fresh look at his boyhood, a man may perceive more clearly who he was as a boy and why he experienced life as he did. He may also reach a deeper level of understanding and appreciation for how his boyhood informed the man he became and also the man that he continues to become. A man's accurate self-understanding has to include an understanding of himself as a boy and how his boyhood continues to affect him. Boys become men, but men always carry within themselves aspects of the boys they once were. Men become better acquainted with and more appreciative of themselves *as men* when they discover more about their boyhood lives. Learning from boys helps facilitate this discovery.

We should also note that when men know themselves better, they have stronger relationships with others, including boys, girls, women, and other men. This fact suggests further that women get to know the men in their lives better and relate to them more authentically and healthfully when these men truly know themselves. It is also the case that women may learn more about the men in their lives by having a richer understanding of boyhood.

It is important for men to revisit their own boyhood experiences through a process of introspection. This process involves reconnecting to their boyhoods through intentional acts of remembering and then speaking (or writing) openly about those memories. I have revisited my own adolescent years to gauge what informed them and how what I experienced affected me, then and in subsequent years. This introspective approach has helped me to delve more deeply into the lives of boys and, by extension, the lives of men.

Some might question whether such an introspective approach could have relevance for making claims about broader boyhood experiences, especially those of contemporary boys, by noting that boyhood today differs from boyhood in the 1950s, 1970s, and 1980s, when the three authors of this book were adolescents. I agree that boyhood is different now, and we do today's boys a disservice if we assume that their experiences are no different than ours were decades ago. All boys live in particular times and places that shape their experiences in distinctive ways. Nevertheless, we can identify commonalities among boys and their experiences that seem to transcend time and place. Boyhood has *not* changed entirely since the three of us were boys. In fact, boys' most basic needs, desires, dreams, and the typical challenges they face endure. As a result, boys of today have more in common with boys of several decades ago than one might initially assume. I recognize this commonality and what it might teach us about today's boys.

By engaging their own histories *and* the boys for whom they care in light of these claims, men and women will become better parents, family members, teachers, coaches, ministers, and friends to boys. With greater understanding of boyhood, adults may discover a deeper degree of empathy and appreciation for the boys they love and seek to support. Men, in particular, will gain a deeper degree of empathy for the boys they were and, in a sense, still are by reconnecting with and understanding the boy-self that continues to live in them. In turn, these adults may gain more emotional accessibility to boys. This accessibility enriches not only the lives of boys but also the lives of anyone who loves and seeks to nurture them. For men who read this book, I would hope that if you have not already done so, "maybe you'll tell your story to yourself, maybe to others" (Dittes 1996, 11). After all, the boy is teacher to the man.

## QUALITIES AND QUESTIONS OF ADOLESCENCE

The psychologist Carl Rogers recognized that "what is most personal is most general" (Rogers 1961, 26). Reflecting on our own experiences and learning from others who reflect on theirs allows a measure of confidence that although we may be different from one another we nevertheless share many common experiences, including similar feelings, thoughts, behaviors, dreams, struggles, and triumphs. A fresh examination of my own adolescent years, conversations with male friends about theirs, and my previous study of adolescence have led me to ponder anew several questions about later adolescence for boys, particularly regarding their friendships. First, what do older adolescent boys want and need that makes for strong bonds forming with peers? For many boys, friendships in adolescence have distinct qualities and a certain type of intensity that subsequent friendships lack. Second, what marks typical late adolescent boys' friendships that results in such potent and long-lasting emotional residue?

### The Value of Distinctions

When exploring the previous questions, and when considering significant needs and desires of older adolescent boys, we must remember that boys differ from one another. Carl Rogers's observations about commonalities among people notwithstanding, we must keep in mind that adolescents make up as diverse a group as any other group. One does well to keep this diversity in mind when considering the lives of adolescent boys. Although we may and should point to boys' common experiences and affirm shared qualities in their emotional and relational lives that link with typical developmental needs and processes, boys remain unique persons. Their experiences vary and remain distinctive, as do their spiritual lives.

The pastoral theologian Emmanuel Y. Lartey provides a helpful way of affirming both commonality and difference among persons. He draws from the work of anthropologist and social theorist Clyde Kluckhohn and psychologist Henry Murray when noting that "every person is in certain respects (1) like all others, (2) like some others, and (3) like no other" (Lartey 2003, 43). As much as individual persons may share in common, they remain different as well. Moreover, differences matter. With respect to boys, their differences matter as much as, and maybe more than, their commonalities.

This last point takes on added importance because a good deal of accepted thinking about boys, many conventional ways of interacting with them, and assumptions about their friendships with one another mistakenly assume minimal differences among them. The quasi-proverbial saying "Boys will be boys" betrays some of these widespread misassumptions. This saying relates to the notion that particular ways of being and behaving, which may involve a measure of mischief, recklessness, and even violence, are normative for boyhood. Other sayings, such as "He's a red-blooded boy" or "He's all boy!" reveal similar beliefs regarding the marks of authentic boyhood. These sayings suggest further that when one of them does not apply to a particular boy—if no one says of him, "He's a red-blooded boy"—then his way of being or behaving falls short of what it should be, and he has in some measure been a failure in his boyhood. Declining to distinguish among boys and their behaviors risks not only misunderstanding boys and their experiences; it also risks *mistreating* them.

We could identify misassumptions and subsequent misunderstandings concerning other groups of people, too, whether having to do with matters of gender, age, race, socioeconomic status, sexual orientation, or most any other identifying characteristic. Truth be told, human beings tend to generalize about people and experiences, often in ways and to degrees that lie beyond conscious thinking. We engage in this generalizing because it requires less mental and emotional energy to assume homogeneity than to recognize differences and adjust our ways of thinking, feeling, and interacting in light of them. In other words, most people find it "natural" to fit people into preconceived understandings of who those people are (or should be) than to allow for more openness and fluidity as concerns personal or group characteristics. Yet acting as if all members of a particular group are in essence alike not only risks missing out on how individuals' distinctive qualities enrich their own lives and those of others; it also fails to honor these individuals and their experiences in ways that prove life-giving for them *and* for others.

Despite similarities among persons, each human being has a unique status tied to a *particular* humanness. Whatever qualities individuals may share with others, they nevertheless *necessarily* remain different from them; they remain unique. I think of God's word to Jeremiah as indicative of this particular humanness that God bestows on all persons: "'Before I formed you in the womb I knew you, and before you were born I consecrated you'" (Jer. 1:5). Differences among persons deserve our devoted attention and high regard, perhaps even more than commonalities. Why? Because our differences, in distinguishing us from others, have a great deal to do with making us who we are, not only in the eyes of other people but in our own eyes and, it would seem, in God's eyes as well.

Differences among older adolescent boys, particularly those differences that a boy may himself recognize and celebrate, also make a boy who he is. Qualities of difference make his *experiences* his own, even when he shares similar experiences with other boys. Qualities of difference likewise inform each boy's status of being *irreplaceable*—of being one of a kind. His irreplaceable nature ascribes a measure of sacredness to him and to his experiences that otherwise would be lacking: "'Before I formed *you* in the womb I knew *you*, and before *you* were born I consecrated *you!*'" Keeping these observations in mind may prevent adults from treating older adolescent boys as if they are all alike, thereby assuaging some of the pressures that boys feel to fulfill expectations tied to being "a real boy."

The last point deserves particular attention. As I noted in our previous book when discussing research on boys and their experiences, and as we also discovered when reflecting on our own boyhoods, boys often become "emotionally *mis*educated" with regard to normative feelings, behaviors, values, and goals. Boys get miseducated about boyhood, which is to say that boys learn erroneous and unnatural ways of being themselves. This miseducation derives from and feeds back into powerful stereotypes of both boyhood and manhood that fail to recognize the distinctiveness of individual boys (and men) and their experiences (Dykstra, Cole, and Capps 2007, 78). Furthermore, these stereotypes, which cannot be separated from the misassumptions about boys and their experiences, get regulated by a potentially destructive set of norms that psychologist William Pollack terms the Boy Code (Pollack 1998, 23–25).

## Residues of the "Boy Code"

The Boy Code consists of the operative norms (values, rules, and expectations) for boyhood in North America, which derive from operative norms of *manhood* that society puts into place and which boys adopt and live by. Parents and other adults adopt and live by these norms as well, expecting that their boys will do the same. As a result, boys feel both internal and external pressures to adhere to these normative feelings, behaviors, values, and goals, not only when these norms feel like a good fit for them but also when they feel unnatural or, worse, impossible to accept. This code operates by virtue of four stereotypes of male ideals and modes of behavior: (1) males should be independent, strong, invulnerable, and stoic; (2) males are naturally macho and full of bravado and are daring, high-energy, aggressive, and even violent; (3) males must achieve power and status and simultaneously avoid shame at all costs; and (4) males do not express thoughts, feelings, or ideals that are "feminine," including dependence, warmth, and empathy (Pollack 1998, 23–24).

These stereotypes and the pressures to uphold them lead to another set of boyhood burdens. Specifically, boys learn to practice "overcompliance" with respect to the expectations of others. A boy learns early in life that meeting others' expectations for him—including those of his peers but especially those of his parents, teachers, coaches, ministers, or other significant and influential adults—may bring rewards of praise, privileges, and safety. A boy also recognizes that failure to meet these expectations, especially those tied closest to what these significant others say that boyhood and manhood require (the most important qualities being nonfeminine ones), leads to criticism, punishment, and even humiliation. Failure to meet expectations may also lead to violence from other boys who want to perpetuate the Boy Code by bullying or physically abusing boys who are perceived as not being sufficiently masculine.

The power that this code wields may be observed in how Ken approached baseball. As humiliating as his experiences playing the game were for him, his *not playing* baseball—which would have meant not complying with expectations put on him by his father and presumably others—would have been worse.[1] So Ken opted to play even though doing so brought its own kind of torment. I believe that Ken had discovered what most boys discover early in life, something that we noted in our previous book. Among the most humiliating insults that a boy receives are being dubbed a wimp, sissy, pussy, homo, or fag, all of which, in his own mind and the minds of others, issue from his being judged as less than fully boy; and "less than" here typically means more like "a girl." Who cannot recall boys who got identified in these ways and the effect it had on how they were treated? My sense is that, for Ken, baseball was what kept these types of insults at bay—insults more painful than the public humiliation of being so awful at baseball.

Adults who do not attend to the distinctiveness of boys' experiences tend neither to recognize these stereotypes nor to challenge them. As a result, these adults uphold the stereotypes and help to strengthen their grip on boys. Let's be clear about some reasons for this result, which may stem from the good intentions that adults have for boys. These adults neither grasp nor celebrate the uniqueness of individual boys because most often the adults themselves were raised with similar expectations, both for boys and for those who seek to support them by helping them become "red-blooded" and "all American." An added rub is that when pigeonholing boys and their experiences, adults may quash a boy's innate motivations for honoring his *own* experiences and the concomitant feelings, behaviors, values, and goals that seem most natural and authentic to him.

## STANDING OUT AND FITTING IN: COMPLEX DESIRES AND NEEDS OF ADOLESCENT BOYS

The psychologist Erik H. Erikson observed that adolescents focus great emotional energy on matters of authenticity and attend especially to working with the tensions between what they want for themselves and what others seem to want from them. As Erikson describes the common experience, adolescents typically become "preoccupied with what they appear to be in the eyes of others as compared with what they feel they are" (Erikson 1980/1994, 94). As a result, when these powerful expectations placed on boys and celebrated by large segments of North American culture feel ill-fitted or unnatural to a boy, and particularly when such expectations constantly beckon a boy for his loyalties, they may come to hold a more defining place in a boy's internal and relational life than his own feelings and desires. When this happens, he lives unnaturally—that is, more by virtue of what others want him to be than by what he wants to be; and living this way usually proves harmful to his emotional, relational, and spiritual life. In other words, boys become overcompliant with regard to the norms and expectations of others, and this overcompliance erodes the boy's sense of being true to who he is. As Teddy describes the struggle and common result, "Most guys don't feel like they can be their own person. . . . It takes a lot to say, 'Oh, I am going to be my own person, and I am not going to try to impress anybody. They can accept me for who I am, and if they don't, then that's their loss'" (Pollack 2000, 42).

A boy's desire to be who he is and to be recognized and even celebrated for it makes me think of Jesus' teaching in Matthew's Gospel about the specialness of individual beings—in this case, sheep. Jesus asks his disciples, "'What do you think? If a shepherd has a hundred sheep, and one of them has gone astray, does he not leave the ninety-nine on the mountains and go in search of the one that went astray?'" Then, regarding the shepherd, Jesus adds, "'And if he finds it, truly I tell you, he rejoices over it more than over the ninety-nine that never went astray. So it is not the will of your Father in heaven that one of these little ones should be lost'" (Matt. 18:12–14). The idea here is that *all* of the sheep are valuable to the shepherd, but also that he values them individually as much as he values them as a group. The shepherd would in fact leave the larger group to seek out a single lost sheep because each sheep is as special—we could even say as sacred—as another.

Later adolescent boys want and need to feel special. They want others, including their parents and other significant adults but also (especially) their friends, to recognize them as distinct individuals precisely because of their unique personal status and value—status and value that they continue to hold on to even amidst the pressures to overcomply with societal norms. This desire to feel special for who they are relates to what might be termed a parallel desire for boys—namely, to enjoy the freedom not to have to comply with norms and expectations of boyhood that feel unnatural or ill-fitting.

I believe that with the baseball team Ken found a group of boys who made him feel special precisely because they liked him for who he was, even though he was awful at baseball. Ken enjoyed a freedom of not having to be good at baseball in order to be liked, which, in a counterintuitive way, provided a salve to the wounds that he surely sustained on the field. Although I'm certain that Ken and the rest of us wished he were better at baseball, I am confident that this would not have made us like him any more than we did. Moreover, I think that, ironically, Ken's being terrible at baseball made him "special" because he and his teammates recognized that he really didn't need baseball prowess to have friends. Being terrible at baseball actually gave Ken a certain (special) type of freedom; he did not to have to comply with regulative boyhood norms linked with being good at sports, and he was liked anyway.

Pollack points out the value of upholding this kind of freedom, as well as the corresponding value of affirming boys for who they *are* as opposed to who they "should" be, when he discusses the role of fathers in their boys' lives. He writes, "As best you can, try to value your sons for who they are rather than for what they do. This means that instead of loving your son based on any particular quality or competency you *wish* he had, ideally you will love him for the qualities and competencies that he already has, those that come naturally to him" (Pollack 1998, 140). I don't know whether Ken's father offered him this kind of love, but I think that his teammates—his friends—did offer it, or we offered a version of it that buoyed Ken and us in ways that made a lasting impression.

Pollack's wisdom must not be missed. Many fathers, because they were raised in the grip of the Boy Code themselves (and this code was stricter for them than it is for boys now), have expectations for their sons that adhere, more or less, to what this code prescribes. If I had to guess, I would say that Ken's father lived with these expectations for Ken, or, if not, Ken thought he did. These expectations may lead fathers to miss recognizing and celebrating their sons for who they are and for what they do, and they may also lead to fathers criticizing their sons for who they are not. When we remember that boys crave acknowledgment and acceptance, not only from their fathers but from all of the significant people in their lives, we glimpse the powerful binds that many boys experience. They want their fathers to love and accept them as they are; they want others to do the same, including mothers, teachers, coaches, ministers, other adults, *and* their peers; yet they also want to be viewed as normal boys. They want a broader range of thoughts, feelings, values, experiences, talents, and goals recognized and affirmed for their intrinsic value, and especially if and when these do not map on to standards prescribed by the Boy Code or its ancillary stereotypes. Moreover, boys want the adults in their lives to be willing to "go the extra mile" for them, particularly when they stray from expectations (and many boys will), precisely because they are valued for their individual, natural, and sacred selves.

Noting the importance of both recognizing and valuing differences among people, Donald Capps points out that in human differences, regardless of their scope, we find what William James calls the "line where past and future meet" (James 1992a, 650; Capps 2001, 247). This line becomes apparent in experiences of losing a loved one to death. As Capps writes, "When we mourn the loss of a loved one we mourn the passing of a person who was *sui generis*, one of a kind. It is perfectly true—not just hyperbole or exaggeration—when the mourners say to one another, 'We will not see the likes of him—or her—again'" (247). Adolescent boys want and need others to recognize them as "one of a kind," the likes of whom will not be seen again, and to relate to them accordingly.

What follows from seeking "one of a kind" status is that most adolescent boys also want to stand out from the crowd in some form or fashion. The degree to which they seek to stand out varies among boys, but most want to be recognized as individually significant and distinctive, whether with regard to appearance; interests; some talent or skill in music, art, sports, academics, or mechanical matters; or some other valued pursuit. Even the shyest of boys will give evidence of this desire to stand out.

This desire to stand out tends to coincide with wanting and needing to "fit in." Adolescent boys strive to fit in with their peers too, and in doing so to claim some common status and experiences, some deep-seated connection. Upholding the value of these parallel desires and seeking to honor the necessary tension between them shows that adults recognize the complexity of later adolescence. In fact, we do boys a disservice when we do not recognize this complexity of desires. We cannot honor boys, nor can we provide for their care, nurture, or thriving, without recognizing their differences, uniqueness, and a corresponding sacredness marking their lives. However, neither can we honor them by discounting their need to fit in and to feel connected to their peers by virtue of commonalities. As Capps notes, "judicious minds" have the ability to value another person's "unique individuality" (246). Judicious minds also have the ability to recognize that distinctiveness does not equate with disconnectedness; in fact, these necessarily remain two sides of the same coin. Older adolescent boys need relationships with adults who have judicious minds. The next chapter provides suggestions for how we adults may become more judicious in ways that benefit boys and, by extension, broader populations.

At the same time, boys share many things in common. Judicious adults do well to pay attention to these commonalities, for they help us better understand boys and, just as important, help us support and nurture them. I have already noted the common boyhood desire and need to feel special and affirmed in one's uniqueness. I want to focus here on two additional common desires and needs among adolescent boys.

First, boys have a desire and need to search for and settle on a deeper understanding of who they are and what they strive to be, at least provisionally. In other words, they want and need an identity. They want and need to discover themselves and, in doing so, to believe in themselves. Second, boys need to believe in significant others and in certain values and ideals that they identify as worthy of their attention and strivings. We may think of a late adolescent boy's search for and settling on an identity, at least provisionally, as requiring him to develop and strengthen these capacities for believing. Let us take a closer look at each of these needs.

## The Need for Identity

Adolescent boys want and need to discover an *identity*. The psychologist Erik H. Erikson, whose pioneering work on the place that identity and identity-related matters hold for human development and thriving, described adolescence as the period "between childhood and adulthood . . . during which a lasting pattern of 'inner identity' is scheduled for relative completion" (Erikson 1980/1994, 119). In other words, in adolescence the various elements that make up rudiments of one's identity converge and come to ascendance, making the discovery of who one is a principal concern for one's life. Truth be told, typical adolescents, including boys and girls, will try on numerous *identities* and may carry these multiple dimensions of themselves for many years beyond adolescence. We should not be surprised if their so-called identity actually consists of multiple identities; in fact, this quality of having fluid and multiple identities marks typical adolescents' experiences. Furthermore, for most people identity remains somewhat fluid throughout life, such that new relationships, experiences, and inner growth continue to shape who we understand ourselves to be. Yet this fluidity especially marks adolescent and early adulthood years. Erikson's use of the term "relative completion" recognizes this fluidity.

Here, I want to stress that older adolescent boys will be interested in the questions and marks of identity like never before. This new interest arises due to rapid and definitive physical changes but also due to greater awareness of and concern for what society wants and encourages boys to be. This new interest in identity also relates to greater awareness of and concern for what we could call the technologies of adulthood—that is, requirements for a meaningful and productive life that include attending to potential jobs or professions, to the prospects of eventually finding a mate and having a family, and to various other social and cultural norms in order to integrate these into one's self-understanding. The questions "What will I be when I grow up?" and "What will I do with my life?" and "Who will I be with?" become more frequent and urgent.

Moreover, later adolescence also typically brings a new kind and degree of psychological complexity and difficulty—which usually link with painful life experiences of adolescence—that makes this new interest in identity and its related matters more acute. Typical later adolescent boys will devote much psychological and spiritual energy to identity-related concerns because, for many boys, it seems as though whoever they understand themselves to be is mysterious, precarious, fragile, or strange.

In *Raising Cain: Protecting the Emotional Lives of Boys*, Dan Kindlon and Michael Thompson suggest that three desires tend to unite boys and to flow through their experiences. These include wanting to love and be loved, wanting to satisfy sexual impulses (first through masturbation and then through partnered sex), and wanting to be manly (Kindlon and Thompson (1999/2000, 195–98). Having already noted a boy's desire for his identity, I want to note an additional desire that unites boys—namely, the desire to believe.

## A Need to Believe

Boys in later adolescence share a desire and need to practice *believing*, to which they also devote much energy. In fact, believing and increasing one's confidence in what one believes remain essential for identity development. Boys want and need to believe in significant other persons but also to believe more than ever before in themselves. Believing in others and believing in himself often links with having identified particular values and ideals that the boy honors and seeks to embrace, which become part of his search for identity.

Psychologist Paul W. Pruyser's influential work in the psychology of religious belief adds perspective to the matter of believing in these ways. He points out a common misconception about belief. This misconception is that one can believe—or be a "believer"—without specifying what one believes in; that is, without naming the objects of belief. When a religious person, for example, asks whether you are a "believer," Pruyser points out that you cannot accurately respond without asking, "A believer in what?" or without citing specifically what you believe *in*. Pruyser seeks to correct this misconception relating to believing. He notes that "any belief is ultimately 'belief in . . .' or 'believing that . . .' and the subject matters of belief and believing are of cardinal importance" (Pruyser 1991, 156).

Later adolescent boys must locate and assess objects in which to believe, and in doing so they must learn to think for themselves, as Gordon Allport notes. But adolescents must also learn to *believe* for themselves. They must, through a more critical eye than ever before, question and alter ways of looking at things. In Allport's language, they must "transform . . . second-hand fittings to first-hand fittings" (Allport 1950, 32), moving from what their parents think and believe to what they themselves think and believe on *their own* terms. They must discover people, ideals, and truths worthy of their belief, and typically they discover these ideals and truths through relationships with people they identify as worthy of their trust. When they find these objects of believing and relate to them over time, they develop further their capacity for "believing in" or "believing that," which in turn informs their growing sense of identity. Corresponding with this identity growth is a boy's feeling of at-homeness in the world *and* an associated trust, mutuality, and benevolent self-image that offer him a sense of living amid a "hallowed presence"—that is, his sense of the presence of the Divine and its good intentions toward him *as a boy*.

Boys want and need to locate objects of faith—that is, people and things to trust and who prove trustworthy, in order to claim these objects for their own—in order to have faith in them. It's a circular process: This claiming (faith) leads in turn to more substantial relationships with these objects of faith. These relationships help confer in the boy a deeper sense of meaning and greater affirmation for who he is because he enjoys deeper relationships with what he believes in and finds worthy of his trust. Ken believed in his friends. He did so, in part, because we believed in him. Our believing in one another fostered a mutual trustworthiness that buoyed us, individually and collectively, amid the struggles of adolescent boyhood. Together, we felt more at home in the world.

Equally important, older adolescent boys must learn to believe in *themselves*. This believing calls for trust that lies beyond what others may or may not help to confer. These boys need to find ways of establishing, maintaining, and, most important, demonstrating to themselves their own trustworthiness and their own worthiness as boys. To say it in a different way, boys need to find ways to live as individuals who warrant the faith that they desire to have in themselves and that they wish others to have in them. Note that boys will not believe in themselves (or in others, for that matter) without being taught (by others and by themselves) how to do so. Therefore, *learning* to believe in themselves, along with believing in others, is a key to spiritual and psychological health. In the next chapter, I suggest how this learning to believe in oneself, in others, and in God is most often fostered by deep boyhood friendships.

# 2

# Friendship as Boyhood Spirituality

Friendships offer a boy numerous benefits, including enhancement of his sense of trust, mutuality, self-efficacy, and a benevolent self-image. In doing so, friendships offer their own sense of hallowed presence in a boy's life. Furthermore, friendships have the capacity to compensate for deficiencies in other relationships, including those with parents or primary caregivers, whether these deficiencies trace to earlier childhood or later. This compensatory power of friendship endures despite the fact that good friends may, at times, argue and even "fall out" for a period of time. In this chapter I suggest ways that friendships may provide for each of these benefits. First, however, I want to reflect further on qualities that may mark a boy's spiritual life—that is, I will suggest the power that friendships hold for an adolescent boy's spirituality.

All boys possess a spiritual center that integrates their interior and relational lives. This personal dimension unites boys throughout history and across cultures. Although the forms of their spirituality differ, and while their spirituality may (and often does) seem unconventional (to them and to others), every boy has a spiritual center that plays a prominent role in his life. Therefore, the spirituality of boys provides them with a unifying force, "some continuity or sameness [that] exists despite all the factors that conspire to make them strangers to one another" (Dykstra, Cole, and Capps 2007, 6).

Boyhood spirituality may be said further to involve a newly discovered "sense of spirit," one marked by "an ineffable sense of vigor, enthusiasm, and excitement" that informs three personal qualities (6). These qualities, discussed in our previous book, include self-awareness, self-transcendence, and self-sufficiency. Although a boy's sense of spirit may manifest itself in other ways, these three ways remain principal ones for most boys. Moreover, boys need to develop these personal qualities in order to flourish in their spiritual lives.

The boy's *self-awareness* centers on newly discovered thoughts and emotions that seem to differ, at least somewhat, from those of other boys, such that these thoughts and emotions appear to the boy as being uniquely his own. The boy's *self-transcendence* relates to his sense that he participates in something much larger and more significant than the ordinary and often problematic world in which he lives. He gathers that he has a place in the broader universe—a place of at-homeness in the cosmos. He also senses that the creator of the universe, or at least some significant part of this universe to which he feels drawn, recognizes and connects with him while also connecting him with all that is and will ever be. A third personal quality informed by his spirituality, a boy's *self-sufficiency*, relates to his deepening sense that, in some situations at least, he has the ability to take initiative, to take care of himself, and to make his own way. He views himself as somewhat self-reliant, and perhaps as increasingly so, but also as *reliable*; and he takes pride in these features of himself (6–9).

Note that younger adolescent boys (ages eleven to fourteen) might not experience these qualities of spirit—their spirituality—overtly or regularly. If you asked a younger boy about his spiritual life, he might not own up to having one, nor offer a clear and confident response to the query. However, a boy's silence about spiritual matters does not mean he lacks awareness of them. Rather, his silence relates often to his sense that what he experiences spiritually falls so far beyond accepted conventions that his spirituality has little, if anything, to do with what others (parents, ministers, teachers, and perhaps girls) would define as spiritual. In other words, although the perceptions that boys have regarding their spiritual lives often silence them on spiritual matters, their silence does not mean that they have nothing to say. Whether they speak of them or not, these qualities of boys' budding spirits mark their lives and shape their experiences in later adolescence (ages fourteen to eighteen) like never before, and they know it. Therefore, it becomes essential for adults to recognize these qualities of boyhood spirituality, to affirm their distinctiveness and their inherent value, and to celebrate their unconventional nature, all of which may foster their growth.

I would also emphasize here that we cannot separate spiritual growth and vitality from psychological growth and vitality—hence my psychospiritual focus. A later adolescent boy, like any other person, remains what we might term a psychospiritual being. When considering his spirituality we must pay close attention to his psychological states and needs, including how these states and needs relate to where he is in his psychological development *as a boy*. As important, we must consider the sociocultural context in which he lives as well as his biological make-up. As I have noted in a previous book on anxiety, whatever their ages "persons are simultaneously religious, spiritual, biological, psychological, emotional, relational, behavioral, and cultural beings" (Cole 2008, 14–15). Attempting to separate any of these aspects of a boy's life and personhood, or to assign more value to one aspect than to others, fails to understand or appreciate the boy in his complexity. In a similar vein, although my primary interest here is a boy's friendships and their relationship to his *spiritual* life, all of these features of boyhood remain interrelated, and thus none may be discounted when considering the spiritual lives of boys.

As concerns the later adolescent boy, his budding sense of spirit relates closely to his new and intensified thoughts, emotions, urges, and behaviors; to his increasing independence and new experiences; and also to the qualities of his relationships. In other words, his budding sense of spirit relates closely to what informs his physical, interior, and relational states. Many of his thoughts, emotions, urges, behaviors, and relational qualities appear for the first time in later adolescence. Or if these have appeared previously, they now often manifest in new and more powerful ways. Their newness and power issue in previously unencountered physical, psychological, and relational challenges that the boy might find painful to endure, but also in opportunities that he may find exciting and meaningful.

I want to highlight here that the boy especially finds opportunities for new ways and degrees of *believing*—a depth of believing that he has yet to experience that includes believing in others, believing in particular values and ideals, and believing in himself as a boy. This newly discovered capacity for belief may bring new energy, excitement, and meaning to his spiritual life.

## FRIENDSHIP'S FRIEND: THE SEARCH FOR IDENTITY

I want to return here to the discussion of identity and belief. Friendship plays a significant role in later adolescence because one's friendships during this period of life inform and are informed by one's need to search for and settle on (at least preliminarily) who one is or wishes to be, which includes forming and maintaining stronger beliefs in oneself and others. Moreover, searching for who one is and wishes to be remains tethered to one's capacity and courage for believing in others, in oneself, and in worthy ideals and goals for one's life.

We understand later adolescent boys, including their experiences and their developmental desires and needs, in light of the work of Erik H. Erikson, who also taught us much about identity formation and development in adolescence. Although his views on identity and other matters have been criticized (see, for example, Gilligan 1982) and revised (see, for example, Capps 2008c), his insights concerning human beings' psychological and relational lives nevertheless have remained instructive over five decades after he presented them. His insights regarding the place of identity formation in adolescence, and perhaps especially for adolescent *boys*, remain particularly significant. Let us take a closer look at his view of identity and the pivotal role that adolescence plays in its formation and maintenance throughout life. Let us also consider his broader life cycle theory of human development, which demonstrates the distinctive qualities of adolescent experiences and how these play a lasting role in adolescents' lives.

## Trust and Faith: Cornerstones of Identity

We might think of the late adolescent boy's strength of *believing* in terms of the capacity for having and maintaining *trust* that issues in *faith*. His faith includes faith in himself—in who and what he is as an adolescent boy—but also faith in others, including who they are or *may be* for him, not only in the present but throughout his life. A later adolescent boy deepens his trust and faith, in others and in himself, through his friendships. I have written elsewhere of the importance of the *early* adolescent boy developing a deep friendship with a special peer—a "chum." This term was coined by psychiatrist Harry Stack Sullivan (1953/1997, 245) in the mid-twentieth century as part of his "interpersonal theory." The term denotes a unique relationship with a significant person with whom the boy chooses to become more intimate and to whom he discloses his most deeply held personal feelings, thoughts, ideas, and dreams. As I pointed out in our first book, a mark of *early* adolescence, in fact, is that with it "comes a kid's new kind of intimacy with other persons, and particularly those he deems to be like himself" (Dykstra, Cole, and Capps 2007, 105). Importantly, in this new kind of relationship with a chum "the early adolescent finds approval from one who values him and finds him appealing, which works against the low regard he may have for himself and believes others have for him" by virtue of failing to meet the social norms and expectations for boyhood (106). Early adolescent boys need chums to help them value and believe in peers who may be trusted to protect and serve the boy's interests.

However, once a boy reaches later adolescence, he needs not only to experience the trustworthiness of his peers; he also needs increasingly to experience himself as trustworthy and thereby to believe more strongly in himself. He needs more *self*-affirmation and higher *self*-regard. These qualities get fostered first in a boy's nurturing early relationships with parents or primary caregivers, in what psychologists refer to as early object relations. But eventually the qualities get fostered in nurturing relationships with other family members and peers. These qualities also get fostered as a boy increases his abilities for self-affirmation—that is, as he comes to rely increasingly on his own sense of personal value, along with relying on others to affirm him. In other words, the later adolescent boy needs to acquire a greater ability for generating and sustaining *internal* supports along with relying on external ones. He needs supports for his boyhood self that link with the act of believing in himself, not merely because others do but because he himself does, on his own terms. He needs an internal (a *self*-evident) basis for confidence in his significance as a boy, one who may follow his own heart and expectations. (Later in this chapter I will say more about how this internal self-regard may grow by virtue of what a boy receives through his friendship.)

We may further distinguish between trust and faith by noting that the latter requires more intentional consideration and reflection. Faith requires conscious and explicit acts of thinking about and assessing the trust that one has, whether in others, in oneself, or in worthy ideals and goals. A boy must, in some form or fashion, become aware of the fact that he trusts, and he must decide whether this trust is warranted. If it is, he moves toward having faith, a deeper and more mature form of trust that can withstand challenges to the security it provides. In contrast, trust, which precedes faith, follows more from prereflective and even unconscious experiences. Whereas we might submit that a baby trusts his caregivers, we would mean something different from claiming that he has faith in them. He might acquire faith in them as he matures, but such faith requires thinking more explicitly about whether one's trust is warranted and how this trust manifests itself in one's life. Nevertheless, although one must trust before acquiring faith, it remains true that as one matures, one's trust may not only inform one's faith, but one's deepening faith may also strengthen one's trust, such that the two qualities, trusting and believing (having faith "in" or "that"), remain mutually informative of each other.

A capacity for trusting oneself and others begins to develop in infancy and continues throughout childhood such that, ideally, late adolescent boys have already acquired some measure of trust that they may continue to draw on throughout the adolescent years and beyond. Trust in infancy and childhood relates to the quality of the relationship between children and caregivers. As Erikson describes this relationship, which he ties particularly to the relationship of infants to mothers,

> . . . the amount of trust derived from earliest infantile experience does not seem to depend on absolute quantities of food or demonstrations of love, but rather on the quality of the maternal relationship. Mothers create a sense of trust in their children by that kind of administration which in its quality combines sensitive care of the baby's

individual needs and a firm sense of personal trustworthiness within the trusted framework of their community's life style. This forms the basis in the child for a component of the sense of identity which will later combine a sense of being "all right," of being oneself, and of becoming what other people trust one will become. (1968/1994, 103)

Although Erikson recognized the indispensible role that mothers play in the lives of their children, and especially nursing mothers of infants, we should understand that the term *mother* may apply as much to the one who provides primary care and nurture as it does to biological mothers. Erikson's primary interest remained with the quality of a person's early significant relationships, represented best by the infant's relationship with its primary caregiver, who in Erikson's time typically was its mother.

Whatever the degree of trust that one develops in infancy and childhood, I would stress that (1) adolescence calls for turning that trust into more mature forms of faith; (2) this effort requires more intentional reflection on and assessment of one's trust; and (3) this reflection and assessment serve to strengthen trust and help a boy enjoy its benefits further.

This movement toward faith also brings about opportunities for increasing spiritual and psychological vitality. In particular, Erikson notes that both people and ideals become the principal objects of faith for the adolescent, and especially as the identity crisis of adolescence ensues. This crisis will be discussed in more detail, but note how Erikson distinguishes between the periods of infancy and adolescence regarding the matter of faith. He writes, "If the earliest stage bequeathed to the identity crisis an important need for trust in oneself and in others, then clearly the adolescent looks most fervently for men and ideas to have *faith* in, which also means men and ideas in whose service it would seem worth while [sic] to prove oneself trustworthy" (128–29).

## Dimensions of Identity

Let us now consider the relationship of identity to the self.[1] Although these two concepts differ in significant ways, Erikson suggests they have often been used somewhat interchangeably, especially in psychoanalytic thought. Noting that identity has been taken to refer to "something noisily demonstrative, to a more or less desperate 'quest,' or to an almost deliberately confused 'search,'" Erikson offers an alternative view consisting of "two formulations" that demonstrate "what identity feels like" when one becomes "aware of the fact that [one does] undoubtedly *have* one" (Erikson 1968/1994, 19).

He appeals to the thought of Sigmund Freud and William James, whom he refers to as "two bearded and patriarchal founding fathers of the psychologies on which our thinking on identity is based" (19). James, he suggests, captures best in a letter to his wife what might be called a *subjective* sense of identity, that is, "a *subjective sense* of an *invigorating sameness* and *continuity*":

> A man's character is discernible in the mental or moral attitude in which, when it came upon him, he felt himself most deeply and intensely active and alive. At such moments there is a voice inside which speaks and says: "*This* is the real me!" (19)

Erikson quotes James further, claiming that

> such an experience always includes . . . an element of active tension, of holding my own, as it were, and trusting outward things to perform their part so as to make it a full harmony, but without any *guaranty* that they will. Make it a guaranty . . . and the attitude immediately becomes to my consciousness stagnant and stingless. Take away the guaranty, and I feel (provided I am *ueberhaupt* in vigorous condition) a sort of deep enthusiastic bliss, of bitter willingness to do and suffer anything . . . and which, although it is a mere mood or emotion to which I can give no form in words, authenticates itself to me as the deepest principle of all active and theoretic determination which I possess. . . . (19)

The subjective sense of identity, which Erikson would also refer to as "I-ness" or "*the pure I*," is characterized both by one's sense of "continuous existence" and by a "coherent memory" (19). Its underlying quality may be recognized by others even when it is not especially conscious to the "I" itself (i.e., self-conscious). As a result, "one can observe a youngster 'become himself' at the very moment when he can be said to be 'losing himself' in work, play, or company. He suddenly seems to be 'at home in his body,' to 'know where he is going,' and so on" (19). For Erikson, this subjective sense of identity is one's *personal* identity.

A second dimension of identity, what Erikson termed the "psychosocial" or "cultural" identity, relates to personal identity but also has distinct qualities (1987a, 675). He appeals to an address by Freud in 1926 to the Society of B'nai B'rith in Vienna to illustrate its characteristics (676). Erikson quotes from this address, in which Freud comments on his Jewish identity:

> What bound me to Jewry was (I am ashamed to admit) neither faith nor national pride, for I have always been an unbeliever and was brought up without any religion though not without respect for what are called the "ethical" standards of human civilization. Whenever I felt an inclination to national enthusiasm I strove to suppress it as being harmful and wrong, alarmed by the warning examples of the peoples among whom we Jews live. But plenty of other things remained over to make the attraction of Jewry and Jews irresistible—many obscure

emotional forces, which were the more powerful the less they could be expressed in words, as well as a clear consciousness of inner identity, the safe privacy of a common mental construction. And beyond this there was a perception that it was to my Jewish nature alone that I owed two characteristics that had become indispensable to me in the difficult course of my life. Because I was a Jew I found myself free from many prejudices which restricted others in the use of their intellect; and as a Jew I was prepared to join the Opposition, and to do without agreement with the compact majority. (1968/1994, 20–21)

As Erikson notes with regard to the original German language in which the address was presented, Freud's mention of "obscure emotional forces" and the "safe privacy of a common mental construction" indicate that these are neither simply mental nor truly private, but rather involve "a deep communality known only to those who [share] in it, and only expressible in words more mythical than conceptual" (21). Along with being subjective (personal), then, identity is also collective (communal) in character. To whatever extent we discover who we are and live accordingly, we do this in the midst of a group of others—a community that confers identities upon its members. Consequently, when thinking about identity, whether for adolescent boys or some other group, we cannot separate either "personal growth" or "communal change," nor the *individual's* identity crisis and broader *sociocultural* crises in history, for "the two help to define each other and are truly relative to each other" (23).

Although Erikson's latest work would focus more heavily on the subjective sense of identity, or "I-ness" (Erikson 1981), and even characterize identity in increasingly mystical terms, he never relinquished the twofold nature of identity that includes both individual and cultural factors. Identity is both individual and psychosocial in scope, "at once subjective and objective, individual and social" (Erikson 1987a, 675). As Erikson commented in *Gandhi's Truth*, such is "the identity of these two identities" (1969, 265–66).

Erikson makes a further distinction between the concepts of *personal* identity and *ego* identity. He suggests that "the conscious feeling of having personal identity is based on two simultaneous observations: the immediate perception of one's selfsameness and continuity in time; and the simultaneous perception of the fact that others recognize one's sameness and continuity" (Erikson 1980/1994, 22). This view of personal identity compares to ego identity, which is the subjective "awareness of the fact that there is a selfsameness and continuity to the ego's synthesizing methods and these methods are effective in safeguarding the sameness and continuity of one's meaning for others" (22). Stated differently, ego identity is the culmination of ego values that accrue in childhood and inform one's "confidence that one's ability to maintain inner sameness and continuity (one's ego in the psychological sense) is matched by the sameness and continuity of one's meaning for others" (94). Hence, the ego serves to "accomplish the selective accentuation of significant identifications throughout childhood and the gradual integration of self-images which culminates in a sense of identity" (Erikson 1968/1994, 209). The difference between *personal* identity and *ego* identity, then, is that whereas the former is concerned essentially with the "mere fact of existence," the latter is concerned with the ego *quality* of that existence. In my use of the concept of identity, both meanings are implied.

## Identity and the Life Cycle

The concepts of "self" and "identity" are intrinsically related, with identity being the self's primary attribute, character, or "substance," as well as its goal. People strive to have an identity, and, for Erikson, the self and its images or representations—via the integrative agency of the ego—culminate in a sense of identity. Such a claim has to be understood, however, in the context of what is said to be identity's "indispensable coordinate," namely, the human life cycle.

Following Freud's insights, Erikson contends that psychological stress or conflict is similar in content to "normative" conflicts that every child must experience and resolve in childhood and whose "residues" all adults carry in the recesses of their personalities (Erikson 1968/1994, 91). This claim informs Erikson's view of eight distinct life stages that collectively make up the human life cycle.

Each life stage involves a "critical psychological conflict" or "crisis" that must be "resolved unceasingly" if the human being is "to remain psychologically alive" (Erikson 1980/1994, 52). The phenomenon is termed a crisis in that "incipient growth and awareness in a new part function go together with a shift in instinctual energy and yet also cause a specific vulnerability in that part" (Erikson 1968/1994, 95). In other words, there is a dialectical tension of sorts between opposing forms of psychic energy that *meet* at a given life stage. Out of this tension, which is always epigenetically driven (i.e., based in one's physical and interior make-up) but likewise influenced by one's socio-cultural milieu (i.e., one's environment), arises a conflict that the individual must resolve. Hence, "crisis" refers to a "turning point," a potentially "radical change in perspective," or "a crucial period of increased vulnerability and heightened potential, and therefore, the ontogenetic source of generational strength and maladjustment" (96). During each of the life cycle stages there is a "focal tension or conflict between a positive, growth-oriented strength and a negative growth-impeding weakness," and healthy growth requires that the individual obtain "a preponderance of the designated strength over the weakness, though the weakness is never entirely overcome" (Capps 1990b, 648). This means that the "ratio of development" should be in favor of the growth-oriented strength if psychological health is to be realized (Erikson 1987b, 596).

With a nomenclature reflecting these respective *crises*, Erikson's life cycle stages include basic trust versus basic mistrust (infancy); autonomy versus shame and doubt (early childhood); initiative versus guilt (play age); industry versus inferiority (school age); identity versus identity confusion (adolescence); intimacy versus isolation (young adulthood); generativity versus stagnation (adulthood); and integrity versus despair (late adulthood).

For Erikson, merely being alive is not to be "healthy" or, as he prefers to say, "vital" (1968/1994, 91). The purpose of his theory of the life cycle, therefore, is to articulate the characteristics that inform a typical pattern of development. Thus, he purports "to describe those elements of a really healthy personality which . . . are most noticeably absent or defective in neurotic patients and which are most obviously present in the kind of [individual] that educational and cultural systems seem to be striving, each in its own way, to create, to support, and to maintain" (Erikson 1980/1994, 52). He formulates a theory of *psychosocial* health or well-being that seeks to demonstrate how the human personality grows or *accrues* "from the successive stages of increasing capacity to master life's outer and inner dangers—with some vital enthusiasm to spare" (53). Fundamental to his theory is the notion that human growth is always grounded in an epigenetic principle or "ground plan" whose teleology (end goal) is based on "inner laws of development" (53). Similarly, the theory is presented "from the point of view of the *conflicts*, inner and outer, which the healthy personality weathers, emerging and reemerging with an increased sense of inner unity, with an increase of good judgment, and an increase in the capacity to do well, according to the standards of those who are significant to him" (52, emphasis added).

Along with this epigenetic ground plan, the individual's life cycle is also shaped by sociocultural influences, what were previously described as psychosocial elements of identity. This means that while its sequence and goal always follow an internal ground plan, the *content* of each life stage and the life cycle as a whole will be "filled out" with regard to the interplay of psychological *and* sociocultural influences and experiences. In other words, the human personality, which is *psychosocial* in nature, develops "according to steps predetermined in the organism's readiness to be driven toward, to be aware of, and to interact with, a widening social radius, beginning with the dim image of a mother [or caregiver] and ending with mankind, or at any rate that segment of mankind which 'counts' in the particular individual's life" (54). Importantly, this development results in each component of the healthy personality—that is, the elements that interact during the respective crises of development—being "systematically related to all the others," and an interdependence of each "on the proper development in the proper sequence" of the others (54). Moreover, each component "exists in some form before 'its' decisive and critical time normally arrives" (54), as each "comes to its ascendance, meets its crisis, and finds its lasting solution . . . toward the end of the stages mentioned" (56).

There is an inherent relatedness between each of the life cycle stages. Nevertheless, the term *cycle* connotes not only this "tendency for individual life to 'round itself out' as a coherent experience," but also its proclivity to "form a link in the chain of generations from which it receives and to which it contributes both strengths and weaknesses" (Erikson 1987b, 598). Not only are the respective stages of the individual life cycle linked, but individual life cycles as a whole are similarly linked to those of both preceding and successive generations. Erikson calls this linking phenomenon the "cogwheeling" of generations (598).

## Identity Crisis—A Mark of Later Adolescence

In his discussion of the concepts of identity and identity crisis as they relate to the life cycle, Erikson notes that in adolescence the issue of identity moves into ascendance: "It is not until adolescence that the individual develops the prerequisites in physiological growth, mental maturation, and social responsibility to experience and pass through the crisis of identity" (Erikson 1964, 152). Adolescents attempt to reconcile for themselves at least two important concerns, including "what they appear to be in the eyes of others as compared to what they feel they are" and "the question of how to connect the roles and skills cultivated [in] earlier [life stages] with the ideal prototypes of the day" (Erikson 1968/1994, 91). Hence, for Erikson, one cannot move through adolescence "without identity having found a form which will decisively determine later life" (128).

I agree with this claim insofar as identity is defined narrowly with regard to its relationship to the influences of ideology, on the one hand, and broader psychosocial dynamics, on the other. Indeed, the *identity crisis* per se remains a hallmark of adolescence and sets the stage for understanding one's identity throughout the rest of life (91). But I would emphasize another aspect of the relationship between identity formation and crisis. This aspect is present during the first life cycle stage and informs the first psychosocial "crisis" to be overcome, namely, a sense of basic trust versus basic mistrust.

In the context of discussing the "ego's beginnings," Erikson suggests that "as far as we know, [the ego] emerges gradually out of a stage when 'wholeness' is a matter of physiological equilibration, maintained through the mutuality between the baby's need to receive and the mother's need to give" (82). The consistency of this mutuality, along with the primary caregiver's own sense of continuity between his or her "biological role and the values of [his or her] community," communicates to the infant that it may trust the caregiver, the larger world, and itself (82). This consistency leads to the infant's forming a basic sense of trust, which is said to be "the first basic wholeness" in that "it seems to imply that the inside and the outside can be experienced as an interrelated goodness" (82). Such trust is said further to involve "an essential trustfulness of others as well as a fundamental sense of one's own trustworthiness" (96) and is "the ontological source of faith and hope" that subsequently emerge from its initial realization (82). The opposite of this sense of trust is a sense of basic mistrust, which is "the sum of all [the infant's] diffuse experiences which are not somehow successfully balanced by the experiences of integration" (82).

The ability to trust determines how an infant will respond to experiences of loss and other life stressors. This is because such losses and stressors of varying degrees and importance may be compensated by the infant's sense of trust in the "interrelated goodness" experienced in the caregiver-infant relationship. Erikson notes a change in the dynamics of the mother-infant relationship during the process of weaning that inevitably involves an infant's sense of stress and loss. But Erikson distinguishes between these typical senses of loss and more traumatic ones, that is, losses in which the "residue of 'basic mistrust'" is deposited and losses over against which a sense of "basic trust must establish and maintain itself" for vital life (101–2). As Erikson suggests,

> A drastic loss of accustomed mother love without proper substitution at this time can lead, under otherwise aggravating conditions, to acute infantile depression or to a mild but chronic state of mourning which may give a depressive undertone to the remainder of one's life. But, even under more favorable circumstances, this stage seems to introduce into the psychic life a sense of division and a dim but universal nostalgia for a lost paradise. (101)

## A Need for Empathic Faces

Erikson's further contention is particularly crucial for my own claims about identity, belief, and friendship:

> The earliest and most undifferentiated "sense of identity" . . . arises out of the encounter of maternal person and small infant, an encoun-

ter which is one of mutual trustworthiness and mutual recognition. This, in all its infantile simplicity, is the first experience of what in later reoccurrences in love and admiration can only be called a sense of 'hallowed presence,' the need for which remains basic in man. (Erikson 1968/1994, 105)

What first constitutes the rudiments of identity are the mutual trustworthiness and recognition provided in the infant's earliest encounters with "mother." Here the infant begins to trust himself and others and therefore to feel at home in the world. *But this is only the beginning.* The infant merely begins a process of identity formation that extends to adolescence and beyond, and which continues to develop throughout the life cycle. This understanding of identity formation suggests that while the identity crisis per se may indeed occur in adolescence, when the individual places faith in people and ideals in order to secure an identity that will continue to inform subsequent psychosocial development, the basis of identity remains grounded in the earliest encounters between the infant and his primary caregiver—that is, the one who consistently provides the infant with an empathic face. Erikson's view also suggests that identity remains closely tied throughout life to one's most significant object relationships, which, for later adolescent boys, includes friendships.

Particularly important for understanding the role of the empathic face as a psychological basis of both identity formation and friendships is what Erikson terms *the morning greeting ritual* between caregiver and child (Erikson 1977, 85-92). The morning greeting ritual involves the waking infant's stirring in the caregiver an array of emotions and affects that are then internalized by the infant—taken in via a sort of mirroring process, so that the child's own ego begins to assume these qualities. Therefore, when a caregiver responds favorably to the infant's appropriately narcissistic demands, that is, when she affirms the child's needs by consistently meeting them adequately, the infant develops a sense of trust, mutuality, and what Erikson calls a "benevolent self-image" (87). Developing these internal traits enables the infant to experience the sense of "hallowed presence" that I have described and also serves as the bedrock of subsequent identity formation and development.

At the same time, the caregiver benefits from this morning greeting ritual such that ongoing encounters become mutually efficacious (Cole 2009).[2] The infant who awakens consistently to the inviting and empathic face of the caregiver internalizes the caregiver's welcoming and comforting affect such that the infant senses safety, security, provision, and being valued and takes these qualities of the encounters into himself. In turn, the infant mirrors back to the caregiver a similar affect and associated emotional benefits, which spawns in the caregiver similar feelings of trust, mutuality, and benevolence. Through these encounters, the infant and the caregiver discover that they need each other; that they rely on each other for a life-giving sense of hallowed presence and at-homeness in the world. This at-homeness and hallowed presence issue from frequent and consistent face-to-face encounters that include responsiveness and support and that literally entail taking parts of the other into oneself and being changed in the process.

## FRIENDSHIP AS A PSYCHOSPIRITUAL STRENGTH

This hallowed presence serves as a prototypical spiritual experience later in life. Why? Because the caregiver enables the infant to experience a deep and abiding trust in one who will consistently provide. At the same time, the infant's reliance on the caregiver meets the caregiver's needs and affirms that adult's purposes as provider. What does this have to do with friendships among boys in later life? I suggest that boys continue to seek these early experiences of a "hallowed presence" that informs "at-homeness" in the world. In fact, boyhood spirituality entails this kind of seeking. Moreover, I suggest that the psychospiritual benefits of these early encounters with empathic caregivers are reexperienced through boys' friendships. Friends offer each other a kind, understanding, and empathic "substitute face"—one that provides assurances that correspond to feeling at home in the world, even amid the precariousness of later adolescence. As a result, friends serve nostalgic *and* compensatory needs in one another's lives. Boyhood friendships provide for reexperiencing the empathic face of a childhood caregiver, for which boys continue to long. At the same time, friends help compensate not only for inadequate early object relations or subsequent poor parenting, but also for the pressures and failures that boys face, whether as a result of the demands of the Boy Code or other difficulties.

I'm suggesting that for older adolescent boys deep friendships provide psychospiritual benefits similar to those of nurturing early object relations between infants and primary caregivers—namely, a sense of hallowed presence in mutuality of recognition, trust and trustworthiness, and a feeling of at-homeness in the world. At any stage of life these benefits, first constituted in the parent-infant relationship, extend dynamically to relationships with others in later life. Moreover, these later nurturing relationships—especially deep friendships—compensate for a lack of mutuality of recognition, trust and trustworthiness, and feelings of at-homeness in the world in earlier relationships.

## Friendships Cultivate Trust and Trustworthiness

Friendships provide a locus for a boy to develop his trust in others, for others to increase their trust in him, and thus for him to have deeper trust in himself. In Erikson's terms, friendships add to a boy's benevolent self-image. As Erikson noted, we learn to trust ourselves by first trusting others. Dynamically speaking, the friend becomes an object of trust that may garner the boy's fidelity as the friend remains true to himself and to the boy. In time, the boy discovers that he has faith in his friend. Analogous to what happens when he experiences consistent nurture and support from his primary caregivers in infancy, friends become objects of his genuine faith that enhance the boy's capacity for and acts of *believing* in others and in himself.

Ken did not believe in himself as a baseball player, but he must have believed in himself as a person because he recognized that he and his friends consistently met one another with empathic faces—affirming and reaffirming one another in our common boyhood. Ken was a giver and receiver of authentic friendship. His friends stuck with him despite the burdens of having a lousy player on their team, and he stuck with them despite their own mistakes and causes for disappointment. We boys genuinely liked Ken for who he was, which offered external affirmations and consolations to assuage the painful effects of his struggle with baseball. I am convinced that it was because he believed in friendship that Ken believed in himself.

Stated a different way, friendships among boys, which involve their own kinds of rituals—including what happens on baseball fields—may serve to extend the psychospiritual dynamics and benefits issuing from the morning greeting ritual. With Ken, our various rituals of friendship (playing baseball, getting burgers and ice cream, spending time in one another's homes), similar to the morning greeting ritual between caregiver and infant that Erikson identifies, provided for consistent nurture and support as he searched for his identity *as a boy*—one who was both "special" (different) and "the same as" other boys—and as he experienced the trust and trustworthiness joined to his boyhood status.

## Friendships Temper the Effects of Not Meeting Expectations

By virtue of being marked by a deep degree of trust, friendships also help temper the pain associated with boys' not meeting expectations (including those driven by the Boy Code) and the associated stereotypes of male behavior that burden boys. As Pollack notes, when boys "feel comfortable that they will not be humiliated by girls or other boys for doing so, many boys derive tremendous joy from participating in a full range of playful, expressive, and creative activities" (1998, 60). Friendships encourage such participation because typical boys, to varying degrees, tend to share with their closest friends parts of themselves (experiences, beliefs, fears, hopes, passions, and vulnerabilities) that may be interpreted by others as inconsistent with being "a real boy." In other words, boys will tend to relax and to risk appearing more feminine with their closest friend, at least when no one else is present, than they will with others, especially those they view as holding undesirable or unachievable expectations for them.

At the same time, as Pollack observes, adolescent boys often feel conflicted about close friendships, as some may be marked by high degrees of trust and intimacy while others are characterized more by competitiveness and even confrontation. We need to recognize the complexity of boys' friendships and also grant that not every friend or friendship provides unceasingly for what a boy may need in the way of affirmation. Nevertheless, most boys desire a "best friend" or two who can be relied on and who view the boy as being himself reliable. A boy discovers that the best friend is one with whom he may be most authentic—most himself—but also one who will maintain fidelity to him precisely *because he is* himself, which includes both his virtues and his need for improvement. As the baseball season with Ken wore on, I recall that he and his teammates were able to engage in some degree of playfulness about his lack of baseball skill, such that what, on the one hand, was the focus of much negative attention and pain became, on the other hand, a means for engaging in boyhood playfulness. For example, before one game Ken said to a star player in front of the team, "The coach told me that I'm starting today and that you're on the bench," to which many of us responded with laughter. On another occasion, a different teammate who was talking about an attractive girl at school said, in front of Ken, "Ken has a better chance at batting .500 than you do with that girl"—to which Ken said, "He's right." Again, the response was genuine levity.

Furthermore, a boy recognizes that as he maintains his own fidelity to his friend, he demonstrates his own trustworthiness, thereby trusting himself more deeply and becoming more who he is or wants to be. In this, he develops his identity. Trusting in others and in himself, which requires demonstrating his own trustworthiness, remains essential for the older adolescent boy.

## Friendships Help a Boy Resist the Pressures to Overcomply

Not only do they temper the tyranny of others' expectations, boyhood friendships also mitigate a boy's propensity for overcompliance with external demands. As Emerson noted, a friend is one with whom a person can be sincere. With friends, boys may relate more from who they authentically are as opposed to what they are expected to be. This means that, together, boyhood friends may choose not to comply with unwanted pressures and demands put on them. In other words, at their best, boys' friendships involve mutually appreciated and mutually supported rebellion. Donald Capps describes his own experience with milder forms of rebellion as an early adolescent:

> What I did not realize at the time is that this rebellious spirit has a positive side. . . . It gives a boy a sense of self-sufficiency, the sense that . . . he has "the necessary resources to get along without help; independent." A boy's rebellious spirit is a reaction to the vicissitudes of adult forms of support and beneficence. By expressing and exercising the spirit of rebellion, a boy discovers that there are limits to how far those who have the power and resources to help and assist him are willing to go. By trying and testing these limits, he becomes more aware of his own power and resources, his own capacities for making good things happen. (Dykstra, Cole, and Capps 2007, 132)

Capps cautions against too much rebellion, however, noting that it may result from a boy's miscalculating his own resources and strengths, and also that it may lead to an "unnecessarily cynical view of adult (and therefore institutional) forms of authority and to the equally inaccurate view that all authority is suspect and unworthy of one's support and confidence" (132).

In light of Capps's observations, I would emphasize the importance of recognizing that "mildly" rebellious behaviors among boyhood friends, especially during later adolescence, help them resist the strong pressures to comply with adult authority that both sanctions and derives from the prevailing stereotypes of boyhood and manhood. Friendships encourage unconventional, and even rebellious, beliefs, behaviors, and goals because friends may feel free to challenge prevailing conventions and authorities, whether parents, teachers, coaches, clergy, or other influential adults. When boys get together, they often engage in talk that relates to rebellious beliefs, behaviors, and goals. Whether these rebellious beliefs, behaviors, or goals are realized in a boy's life or not, simply broaching them and fantasizing about them with a close friend allow a boy to imagine a world in which he could feel freer to be himself. As he dreams about that life, he may find more courage to live it, or to approximate it, in ways that prove life-giving to him. Mild forms of rebellion that take place in the context of friendships also allow a boy to "stand out" from the crowd while also remaining one who "fits in," at least with his friends. A boy recognizes that these friends affirm his unique individuality but also claim with him common status, experiences, and deep-seated connection. In these friends a boy places his trust and faith.

## KEN'S HAPPY ENDING

Ken's story has a happy ending. At the next game, the penultimate inning came, and Ken was inserted dutifully into the lineup, once again to comply with league rules. As we were the home team that day, he began the inning in right field and had no balls hit to him—thank God. When it was our team's turn to bat, he was second in the order. The boy who batted before him had gotten on base with a walk. As Ken approached the batter's box, my thoughts returned to the previous game and to the anguish of his last time at bat. I remember praying that he would get a hit. I suspect that many others prayed for this, too. No one must have prayed harder than Ken. On the very first pitch, Ken swung the bat but missed. The same thing happened with the second pitch. But on the third pitch, he swung the bat and made contact with the ball. It's still difficult to believe what happened next. Almost as if by divine intervention, the ball blooped into right field! With eyes as large as saucers, Ken ran to first base on his tiptoes, his long arms pumping as his gangly body worked to stay upright, and he touched the base before being called out for the first time all year.

The expression on Ken's face told the story, one that remains embossed in my memory. Amidst failure after failure after failure, he kept trying until he got that first hit. When he finally got on base, it was as if he'd gotten the winning hit in the World Series, for him and for the rest of us. It was all that his teammates could do not to swarm the field in celebration. When another teammate got a hit and Ken crossed home plate to score, however, the entire team gathered around him. With the jubilance of boys we all surrounded him in a circle that quickly enclosed with him at the center. We shouted, "Ken! Ken! Ken! Ken!" Ken held his arms high in the air and held his head almost as high. His teammates' arms were now around him and one another. A pervasive joy hovered over the place for several minutes, and no one wanted it to end. I had the sense that even the opposing team enjoyed this moment. I also had a palpable sense of God's compassion that day and also of God's goodness, and I was grateful.

It has been decades since I last thought of Ken. Yet my eyes moisten when I think about him now—his struggle *and* his hit at the end of the season. Perhaps I look back on that story as much with the eyes of a parent as with the eyes of a boy. The struggles of children become more intense, it seems to me, after one becomes a parent. At any rate, Ken's experience appears to point to the value of persistence and hard work, a virtue that most of us want to uphold and certainly to instill in our children. His story also highlights the value of remaining steadfast in the face of defeat, urging that as we encounter hardships in life, we wipe away our tears and keep stepping up to the plate.

This steadfastness, too, may be virtuous. But as virtuous as any of that were the friendships that Ken enjoyed, relationships that made the challenges that came with failing so miserably at baseball tolerable because what friends provided him was so deeply empowering.

It's also the case that Ken's story has a happier ending than do some similar stories; not all stories end so favorably. While celebrating his triumph we remember the boys who *never* get that single hit and who never experience a measure of success or affirmation that serves to assuage, at least for a few moments, the pain tied to feeling like a consummate failure. When a boy fails to measure up to these norms and expectations, he experiences shame and injury to his self-confidence because he suffers injury to his deepest self—the core of who he understands himself to be or wants to be, however rudimentary his self-understanding may be. Furthermore, the damage from this self-injury that ensues may not be undone by the success a boy enjoys. The seemingly constant pressure of living against the backdrop of unachievable norms and expectations, whether those of others or one's own, proves destructive. The residue of these negative experiences gets lodged deep within oneself and serves to temper confidence that comes with success.

However, as is true for early adolescent boys, the later adolescent boy need not have all positive experiences in this period of life—indeed, what boy could?—in order to fare well spiritually. He need not have all positive experiences in order to foster his spiritual life, including his capacities for self-awareness, self-transcendence, and self-sufficiency, and to believe in others, in himself, and in worthy ideals and goals. Similar to their younger selves, most older adolescent boys have positive and negative experiences—joys and pains—and many boys may have more of the latter than the former, one reason that scores of adults look back on their high school years in particular with as much ambivalence as attraction. As the poet and critic John Ciardi noted, "You don't have to suffer to be a poet. Adolescence is enough suffering for anyone" (in Vecchione 2007, 99). I recall, too, that when I mentioned to a colleague that I was working on chapters for a book that involved reflecting back on my adolescence and examining those years more closely, his facial expression changed noticeably and he said, "I'm sorry. I feel badly for you now . . . but better you than me!" Many adults will understand his sentiments. So, too, will many adolescents.

The challenges typical to adolescence notwithstanding, *both* types of experiences, positive and negative ones, are essential for helping a boy understand himself, what he desires and values, and whom he seeks in his relationships. In other words, a range of experiences shapes boys as persons, and necessarily so—which means that both positive and negative experiences hold value for a boy's *spiritual* life. An adolescent boy may grow as much in his self-awareness, self-transcendence, and self-sufficiency—as well as in his capacities for believing in ways mentioned—when failing at a sports event (an experience that he would deem negative and undesirable) as he does when succeeding in a challenging course at school (an experience that he would deem positive and desirable). In fact, I doubt if Ken would have been embraced by his teammates to the extent that he was had he been merely average at baseball. Nevertheless, whereas our focus in the previous book on the *early* adolescent boy and his spiritual life highlighted the particularly powerful role played by experiences that he would deem negative and undesirable, I want to highlight here the role that positive and desirable experiences issuing from deep friendships may play in the *later* adolescent boy's spiritual life, particularly in light of a typical boy's struggle with being a boy.

## CONCLUSION

What might we learn about later adolescent boys and their spiritual lives from Ken and his friendships? We learn at least this: these boys should be supported in their friendships. Precisely because they allow boys to develop psychospiritual strengths tied to acts of believing in others, themselves, and in worthy ideals (like persistence, courage, integrity, fidelity, and friendship itself), friendships foster a boy's discovery and celebration of his identity and value as a boy. Friendships, at their best, allow a boy to discover and live his most authentic self, even when that self does not map on to expectations operative in his life. Moreover, because acts of believing hold such a central place in a later adolescent boy's life—that is, because he searches for what and in whom he may authentically believe like never before—those who nurture these boys within communities of faith have a particular opportunity. Where believing in God orients life, we may help boys recognize and claim for themselves identities tied not only to friendships but to an even greater "hallowed presence" that proves trustworthy and provides recognition. That source, which draws on a boy's sense of the divine and its good intentions toward him *as a boy*, sustains him—come what may.

# PART II

# Subversive Friendships

ROBERT C. DYKSTRA

# 3

# Subversive Friendships

Sherman Alexie's (2007) novel *The Absolutely True Diary of a Part-Time Indian*, winner of the National Book Award for Young People's Literature, centers on a mostly autobiographical account of a tragicomic rift between Alexie and his best friend and soul mate at age fourteen. The rupture in their friendship comes in the wake of Alexie's decision to attend an all-white high school some twenty-two miles off their Spokane reservation. Its protagonist (and Alexie's alter ego) is Arnold Spirit Jr., a skinny boy mocked by peers and prone to seizures as a result of having been born with excess cerebral spinal fluid ("water on the brain," Arnold calls it).

In the book's final chapter, Arnold reflects on a memory of an earlier time when his friendship with Rowdy, the toughest boy on the reservation and Arnold's fierce defender, was less encumbered. He recalls a hot summer day when he and Rowdy, at that time both ten years old, hiked out past Turtle Lake and saw a pine tree towering one hundred, maybe one hundred and fifty, feet in height:

> "I love that tree," I said.
> "That's because you're a tree fag," Rowdy said.
> "I'm not a tree fag," I said.
> "Then how come you like to stick your dick inside knotholes?"
> "I stick my dick in girl trees," I said.
> Rowdy laughed his ha-ha, hee-hee avalanche laugh.
> I loved to make him laugh. I was the only one who knew how to make him laugh.

Rowdy then proposes that the two of them climb the tree. Though Arnold believes that this could only lead to certain death, he also knows that the nature of their friendship prevents him from backing down from Rowdy's challenge. So they climb the tree, coming within ten feet of the top, swaying with the thin branches in the breeze. From that vantage point they can see for miles:

> "Wow," I said.
> "It's pretty," Rowdy said. "I've never seen anything so pretty."
> It was the only time I'd ever heard him talk like that.
> We stayed in the top of the tree for an hour or two. We didn't want to leave. I thought maybe we'd stay up there and die. I thought maybe two hundred years later, scientists would find two boy skeletons stuck in the top of that tree.
> But Rowdy broke the spell.
> He farted. A greasy one. A greasy, smelly one that sounded like it was half solid.
> "Jeez," I said. "I think you just killed the tree."
> We laughed. And then we climbed down. (226)

Richard Coble, a student in my course on adolescents, contrasts this conversation between ten-year-old boys to the difficulties with intimacy in same-sex friendships that they and other boys will face as they move further into adolescence and adulthood. He writes,

> This conversation, where two boys allow each other to be sensitive in front of one another, to appreciate beauty and to share it with another male, exemplifies the intimate friendships that most men lack because they have repressed the part of them that is attracted to and wants to be comrades alongside other males. At the same time, [Arnold's] and Rowdy's humor around the latter's flatulence allows them to appreciate one another's bodies, to realize that they are both grotesque, organic creatures with needs, desires, and gas. (Coble 2010)

Coble names here the increasing sense of menace felt in shared moments of intimacy between older adolescent boys and between young men. He likewise recognizes the benefit of male humor, especially bodily and sexual humor, for helping attenuate these tensions for boys and men of any age. These insights speak to key interests of this and the following chapter.

But in addition to exploring and seeking to better understand the escalation of these tensions as boys mature, I will also consider here how despite, or because of, these increasing complexities, their friendships constitute the most formidable, redemptive, and easily overlooked component of the spiritual journeys of older adolescent boys. At some level, their friendships actually *are* their spiritual life. Friendships become clear windows into and the most tangible expressions of the spiritual pilgrimages of older boys. Though typically cloaked in humor and often viewed with suspicion by adults, these friendships—rare, guarded, funny, fraught, and subversive—constitute the essence of the spirituality of older adolescent boys.

Alexie captures this intensification as Arnold, now fourteen, breaks the difficult news to Rowdy of his decision to transfer from their deficient reservation high school to an all-white school in another town, effectively condemning Rowdy to a hopeless future on the reservation without Arnold. As Arnold does so, their friendship takes a harrowing turn.

Arnold finds Rowdy alone near the school, noting that his being alone was not unusual given that "everybody was scared of him":

> "I thought you were on suspension, dickwad," [Rowdy] said, which was [his] way of saying, "I'm happy you're here."
> "Kiss my ass," I said.
> I wanted to tell him that he was my best friend and I loved him like crazy, but boys didn't say such things to other boys, and *nobody* said such things to Rowdy.
> "Can I tell you a secret?" I asked.
> "It better not be girly," he said.
> "It's not."
> "Okay, then, tell me."
> "I'm transferring to Reardan."
> Rowdy's eyes narrowed. His eyes always narrowed right before he beat the crap out of someone. I started shaking. (Alexie 2007, 48-49)

Arnold is shaking for good reason, for once Rowdy determines that his friend is not joking, he becomes enraged, stands up, and spits on the ground. Arnold reaches out to touch his shoulder, and Rowdy spins around in response and shoves him:

> "Don't touch me, you retarded fag!" he yelled.
> My heart broke into fourteen pieces, one for each year that Rowdy and I had been best friends.
> I started crying.
> That wasn't surprising at all, but Rowdy started crying, too, and he hated that. He wiped his eyes, stared at his wet hand, and screamed. I'm sure that everybody on the rez heard that scream. It was the worst thing I'd ever heard.
> It was pain, pure pain. (52)

Once again, Arnold reaches out to try to repair the damage. Once again, he touches Rowdy, realizing too late his mistake as Rowdy punches him hard in the face:

Bang! I hit the ground.
Bang! My nose bled like a firework.
I stayed on the ground for a long time after Rowdy walked away. I stupidly hoped that time would stand still if I stayed still. But I had to stand eventually, and when I did, I knew that my best friend had become my worst enemy. (48–53)

With this encounter, Alexie sets the stage for his raw and affecting account of the perilous undercurrents of the friendships of older boys.

Like Alexie, David B. Wexler (2009), a clinical psychologist who writes extensively on psychotherapy with men, observes a related pattern of attenuated self-expression and increasing equivocation in his own adolescent son's friendships with other boys:

My son is, at the time of this writing, 17 years old. One of the true joys in my life used to be watching the delight he experienced with his male friends. He loved them. He lit up when he saw them and even when he was telling stories about them. He would come home and relate a goofy story or joke from one of his pals and he would get a dreamy look in his eyes, as if this friend was just the coolest guy in the whole world. I watched and listened with envy, knowing how hard it is for boys and men to express so much delight with anyone except a lover. Until he hit puberty—and suddenly his responses to his friends were muted, characterized by consciously lowering his voice and grunting noncommittally. To express more would be a violation of the code. It would be too vulnerable. It would be girlish or even (the worst male code violation of all!) "gay." (2)

Wexler appears to resign himself, rightly, in my view, to the inevitability of this increasingly precarious posturing around their male friends as boys approach adulthood. But recognizing its inevitability does not diminish his need to mourn it. He knows that not only his son but he himself and nearly every other boy and man are losing something exceptional as they forfeit expressions of intimacy shared openly by younger boys. Wexler, like Arnold's friend Rowdy, has reason to mourn, even to scream in pure pain, in the wake of this irrevocable loss.

The emotional perils but also the clandestine spiritual possibilities inherent in precisely these sorts of shifts in the ways that older adolescent boys negotiate their friendships, important concerns of the whole of the present book, find particular emphasis in chapters 3 and 4. In these chapters I attempt to show how the spiritual journeys of older adolescent boys may be recognized, encouraged, and sustained with the help of wise companions— those like Alexie, Wexler, and many others we will consider—whose keen understanding of the perils and possibilities of male friendships will help them navigate, and perhaps even subvert, certain stifling masculine norms of church and culture.

## FRIENDSHIP AS SPIRITUAL VOCATION

In his book *Deep Gossip*, literary critic Henry Abelove (2003) recounts an elegy offered by Allen Ginsberg (1996) for his friend Frank O'Hara in the wake of the latter's accidental death at Fire Island in 1966. O'Hara was a curator at the Museum of Modern Art, and in his elegy, Ginsberg described his friend as a "curator of funny emotions" and went on to draw attention to O'Hara's *ear*, "'a common ear,' Ginsberg wrote, 'for our deep gossip'" (191).

Abelove borrows from Ginsberg's elegy the title for his book on the cultural politics of sexuality. In its introduction, he finds continuing resonance in these two curious phrases from this "long-ago" elegy. He writes, "In Ginsberg's terms of description for O'Hara—*Curator of funny emotions, a common ear for our deep gossip*—I believe I hear the intimation of an intellectual vocation. For me, this vocation is an aspiration rather than an achievement" (xii). Though it is unlikely that the intellectual vocation Abelove had in mind was that of a pastoral theologian, I find in his brief exegesis of Ginsberg's words a promising way to describe what in my own work I aspire to be and do. It is also, I'm convinced, a fine way to envision the work of youth ministry with older adolescent boys.

But I choose his words as a foundation for the present chapter as a way not only to think about the vocations of pastoral theologian and youth minister but to consider a calling far more sweeping and familiar, though one perhaps equally imperiled and at least as subversive, namely, the vocation of close same-sex friendships among adolescent boys. I want to suggest that male friends, like professional pastoral theologians and youth ministers, function at their best as curators of funny emotions with a common ear for our deep gossip. Close same-sex friendships, however baffling and elusive for adolescent boys and men, are perhaps their most reliable means of subverting familiar humiliations wrought both by the many institutions they serve and by some uncomfortable psychosocial realities unique to the experience of being male.

## CURATOR OF FUNNY EMOTIONS

Abelove begins his introduction to *Deep Gossip* by pointing out that the word *curator*, in Ginsberg's phrase "curator of funny emotions," derives from the Latin *cura*, meaning "care" or "concern" (and reminiscent, we might add, of a historic understanding of pastoral theology as the art of the "care of souls"). Though O'Hara was a museum curator, Ginsberg broadens the term's meaning here beyond the caretaking responsibilities of those who work in museums or, say, in rare-books rooms or as keepers of zoos. Rather, Abelove suggests, Ginsberg uses the term to "encompass a whole life's work" (xi).

But wouldn't it be demeaning, he proceeds to wonder, to describe intellectuals like O'Hara as mere curators or caretakers rather than "as creators, or as innovators, or as discoverers or expounders of truth, or as contributors to knowledge or understanding, or as contenders against falsehood or ignorance"? Abelove responds by noting that the work of a curator in no way excludes these roles, given that effective caretaking often requires a need to be innovative or contentious. But the word *curator* nevertheless places the emphasis elsewhere, on what seem to be the less glamorous, more self-effacing tasks of "conservation, nurturance, [and] scrupulosity." A curator more often modestly cares than miraculously cures.

What, then, of "funny emotions"? What is a curator of funny emotions? Abelove points to two meanings of the word *funny*. "Emotions are funny," he writes, "when, on the one hand, they are associated with fun or pleasure, and when, on the other, they are likely to be made fun of—mocked, derided, trivialized, even stigmatized" (xii). Because this latter kind of funny emotions touches the most sensitive parts of our lives and can elicit deep shame, such emotions therefore require great care. "To take care of them is, however, to do something different from therapy," Abelove says, "and the word 'curator' points to the difference sharply. Curating, taking care of, isn't curing—or wanting to cure—or supposing or imagining that a cure is needed" (xii). A curator of funny emotions, rather, is one who somehow remains present and accompanies another in facing, and ultimately owning and even honoring, the psychosocial terror, abomination, isolation, or shame that attend a person harboring funny emotions.

## A COMMON EAR FOR OUR DEEP GOSSIP

Ginsberg likewise memorialized his friend as having "a common ear for our deep gossip" (191). Abelove takes the phrase "a common ear" here to mean "a capacity and willingness to listen with close attention democratically, for instance, to all those high or low, extraordinary or ordinary, within one's own circle and kind, or outside of both, who experience and express funny emotions and with them make lives" (xii). A common ear is a democratic ear, an unpretentious ear, a generous and empathic ear attuned to those marginalized by funny emotions and therefore liable to neglect the rich potential found therein.

A common ear, then, for what exactly? For "our deep gossip," Ginsberg says. But can one's attending to gossip be considered anything but a degrading pastime? Are curators of funny emotions supposed to share the kind of ear prized and exploited by the tabloids or the paparazzi? Abelove's response to both of these questions would be a qualified yes, especially if the gossip to which one attends is *deep*: yes, attending to gossip is in some instances important; and therefore, yes, it may be possible for curators of funny emotions to learn something from the tabloids (see, for example, Capps 1998, 173–201; and Schweitzer 2008, 191–203). Why? Because, Abelove writes,

> gossip is illicit speculation, information, [or] knowledge [that is] *an indispensable resource for those who are in any sense or measure disempowered*, as those who experience funny emotions may be, and [such gossip] is deep whenever it circulates in subterranean ways and touches on matters hard to grasp and of crucial concern. (xii, emphasis added)

To care for those who at times cannot even identify, but who more often cannot give voice to, their funny emotions for fear of reprisal in the corporate sphere or public square is to attend to how such feelings find alternate outlets, whether via underground networks, unconscious symptoms, or inarticulate stammering for the elusive right words. To attend to deep gossip is to begin to reclaim what matters most from those high or low whose funny emotions defy cultural conventions.

*A curator of funny emotions with a common ear for our deep gossip*: one would be hard-pressed to find a richer intimation of the vocations of the pastoral theologian and Christian youth worker—caretakers of subterranean emotions and desires that are mocked or trivialized in the social arena but that, when invoked, allow for a fuller expression of who a person really is. To become this kind of curator, as Abelove claims, is typically more aspiration than achievement. But it is a worthy aspiration, one suitable not just for those rarefied birds of pastoral theologian, youth minister, and social critic but for a much broader swath of humanity as well—for example, nearly all older adolescent boys who seek out but also find themselves unsettled by the thought and the experience of intimate same-sex friendships. At their best and, as we shall see, at their most threatening, such friendships press adolescent boys to become curators of funny emotions with a common ear for their friends' deep gossip.

## BODY PARTS

Just what exactly are the funny emotions that attend close same-sex friendships between older adolescent boys? How is it that ordinary friendships can give rise in older boys to concerns of being mocked or stigmatized in the social arena or lead them to underground forms of communication or to deflecting complex feelings from conscious awareness? What leads Arnold to tell Rowdy to "kiss his ass" rather than that he "loved him like crazy"? What is behind the consciously lowered voice or noncommittal grunts of Wexler's seventeen-year-old son? What links everyday male friendships to the funny emotions and deep gossip of which Ginsberg speaks?

These questions cover complex psychosocial terrain that I attempt to navigate in this and the following chapter. Despite these complexities, however, what may be striking is how readily almost any schoolboy over the age of six, if asked about the link between same-sex friendships and funny emotions, would be able to respond with dead-on accuracy. Even without benefit of books like this on the subject, most boys reflexively know that the connection somehow has to do with not wanting to appear vulnerable, dependent, feminine, queer, or gay in relation to another male. For as Jason Taylor, the thirteen-year-old protagonist of David Mitchell's novel *Black Swan Green*, observes, "It's all ranks, being a boy, like the army" (Mitchell 2006, 5). Close same-sex friendships threaten to awaken in boys and men a deep-seated fear of the feminine—of falling too far down in rank—that calls for their constant, though not always conscious, vigilance and defense.

In a newspaper article recounting recent suicides of adolescent boys who were taunted by peers for "feminine" interests such as playing the piano, *New York Times* columnist Judith Warner (2009) writes,

> It's really about showing any perceived weakness of femininity, by being emotional, seeming incompetent, caring too much about clothing, liking to dance or even having an interest in literature. . . . The message to the most vulnerable, to the victims of today's poisonous boy culture, is being heard loud and clear: to be something other than the narrowest, stupidest sort of guy's guy, is to be unworthy of even being alive. It's weird, isn't it, that in an age in which the definition of acceptable girlhood has expanded, so that desirable femininity now encompasses school success and athleticism, the bounds of boyhood have remained so tightly constrained?

Warner quotes Barbara J. Risman, a sociologist at the University of Illinois at Chicago, who says of her own research on boys, "It was just like what I would have found if I had done this research 50 years ago. [Boys are] frozen in time" (see also Blow 2009, 2010). Boys of all ages feel compelled to live with, and some at times die from, these kinds of sobering constrictions.

In his own lifetime, Sigmund Freud was as engrossed by the consequences of this aversion to all things feminine in boys and young men as Warner and Risman find themselves today. Unlike Warner and Risman, however, he would not have been surprised by its intractability, that is, by the masculine time warp of which they speak. He called this defensive posture in boys and men "castration anxiety," an archaic term that may sound quaint or even amusing to the contemporary ear. But to those boys and men who know what Freud was talking about—at some gut level every boy and man—this funny emotion is no laughing matter. They sense its presence on a daily basis in countless social interactions and in palpable intrapsychic tensions.

Freud wrestled for decades in trying to understand the origins and impact of this anxiety in himself and others, not merely in the literal sense of the toddler boy's fear of losing his own penis on discovering that girls somehow have lost theirs, but more expansively at the level of boys' and men's fear of passivity around other males or of their fear of the feminine in countless other guises. In one of Freud's last technical papers on psychoanalysis, "Analysis Terminable and Interminable" (1937/1964), published near the end of his life, he again raises but then essentially throws in the towel over this question. He asserts in the essay's telling conclusion that the fear of passivity among boys and men—what he calls the repudiation of the feminine—is the very "bedrock" of the male soul or psyche, the foundational anxiety beneath which, he believes, no psychotherapy, even his own, can reach or heal. Psychoanalysis, he appears to be saying here, is incapable of penetrating men's fear of being penetrated.

Though few psychoanalysts today share Freud's therapeutic pessimism in this regard, with few exceptions they do agree with him that castration anxiety is ubiquitous (Cooper 2005, 150). Indeed, how could they not? "That castration anxiety continues to occupy a special place, at least in conscious thinking," writes Arnold M. Cooper (2005) in his influential essay "What Men Fear: The Façade of Castration Anxiety," "is as evident to any clinician as it is to the man in the street" (153). But Cooper argues that it is not because castration anxiety is the impassable foundation of all analyzable fears, as Freud claimed, but rather because it is the *least* feared of young children's greatest fears. The anxiety around losing his penis functions for the boy as a relatively wieldy stand-in for far more archaic and menacing terrors much less likely to rise to his conscious awareness. It is "a less fearful disguise," Cooper says, "for other kinds of fear" (153).

Castration anxiety appears in the young boy's life around the same time he is learning to speak and thus can begin to verbalize his fears for the first time. To be able to name his fear of losing a prized body part becomes a way to defend against more severe preverbal, therefore inarticulable, earlier threats. Cooper points out that Freud himself eventually included among the most primitive of a young boy's fears the anxiety surrounding the potential loss not just of his penis but of his mother or her empathy and love, as well as the fear of an excessively punitive conscience or superego (151). Cooper concludes that "while psychoanalytic researchers have differed in their view of what is the basic fear or the sequence of fears, there has been almost no disagreement concerning the special significance of castration fear and the castration complex in shaping male behavior" (153).

As the anxiety closest to the surface of consciousness of a boy's—and later a man's—most traumatic fears, castration anxiety keeps the problem, so to speak, within his grasp. "Terrifying as it is," Cooper says, "the loss of the penis is still only a loss of a part of oneself, a relatively small loss compared with the still-active fears of pre-Oedipal total annihilation," meaning the loss of the boy's mother and her source of love and sustenance, but in addition, I will claim below, the loss of his father as well (154). For Cooper, "what is observed later as castration anxiety"—particularly for our purposes an older adolescent boy's fear of vulnerability in the presence of another male—"is often a desperate attempt to 'escape forward,' as it were, to more advanced levels of representation, escaping from the more primitive and frightening versions of narcissistic threat" (155).


## THE GREATEST OPPRESSION OF BOYS AND MEN

How, then, do these desperate attempts to "escape forward" from literally unspeakable terrors affect adolescent boys' everyday lives and relationships? What do the funny emotions associated with what Freud provocatively called castration anxiety have to do with close same-sex male friendships? If, as Freud believed, this onerous bedrock of male anxiety resists all manner of *cure*, could it possibly become subject, at least, to some manner of *care*? What would be involved in aspiring to become a *curator*, of sorts, of castration anxiety? Through conservation, nurturance, and scrupulosity, would not such a curator somehow seek to explore and conceivably honor, rather than try to eradicate, the special province of the repudiation of the feminine in the life of the ordinary adolescent boy or young man in the street? Would not a curator give ear to its deep gossip even while attempting to contain its harmful fallout?

Near the end of his essay "Men and Christian Friendship," a trenchant and moving historical and pastoral account of how Christian theology has contributed to making male friendship seem "homosexually dangerous" and therefore a "near-impossibility" for older boys and men, Philip L. Culbertson (1996) soberly observes that *"men's fear of intimate male friendship is one of the most critical forms of oppression under which they live"* (174, emphasis added). Culbertson, an American pastoral theologian who taught for many years in New Zealand, has written extensively on men's issues, including men's difficulties with same-sex friendships. His essays on friendship invariably include discussions of threats posed to adolescent boys and men by the specter of homosexuality (Culbertson 1992, 88–89, 103–6; 1994, 73–75; 1996, 163–64). At the heart of their fear of friendship, according to Culbertson, is male homophobia, the fear of those like oneself who are attracted to persons like oneself and therefore, one could say, a form of self-hatred. Or as the British psychoanalyst Adam Phillips deftly asks, "What is so distasteful about one's own sex that one has, so exclusively, to desire the opposite one?" (Phillips 1995, 24).

Culbertson sees homosocial anxiety as taking three specific forms, namely, a boy's or man's *fear of being out of control of his body*, particularly of being unexpectedly aroused; *his fear of vulnerability to other males*, especially of finding himself emotionally in a "one-down" position; and *his perceiving intimacy as claustrophobic*, whereby a boy or man with a "limited emotional repertoire" expends so much energy suppressing his own feelings that he cannot imagine the added burden of having to sustain those of anyone else (Culbertson 1994, 74–75).

A recent controversial advertising campaign for Nike's Hyperdunk basketball shoes managed to capture in a single image and tagline something of all three aspects of this particularly male anxiety—homoerotic arousal, vulnerability, and claustrophobia. The billboards, strategically located near streetball courts around New York City, showed a basketball player getting dunked on by another player. As blogger Hamilton Nolan (2008) describes it, the dunker is hanging off the rim, "his balls dangling in the face of the man being the dunk-ee." Overlaying the photo is the campaign's slogan "That Ain't Right!" Nolan notes that the ads depict what is widely perceived "to be the most humiliating possible thing that can happen to someone on a basketball court" and that the "humiliation arises from the balls-in-face aspect of the dunk." He notes that while hardcore fans of New York streetball "would scarcely think twice about these ads," since trash talk is a fundamental part of the game, "the larger point is that the joke here—as in other campaigns revolving around *all of America's most popular sports*—is based on the implacable homophobia of straight jocks. . . . The sad part is that this *isn't* a new low in homophobic advertising. It's the sports status quo" (emphasis in original). But this campaign is merely one in an unrelenting stream of messages that target young men's fears of physical arousal, emotional vulnerability, and claustrophobic self-depletion. These anxieties coalesce, for Culbertson, to form the harsh vacuum of isolation of adolescent boys and men.

The travail of boys and men around befriending other boys and men may strike some observers as a relatively trivial form of oppression, given long shadows cast by many other forms of human misery. But Culbertson would counsel against dismissing it out of hand. Not only is the repudiation of the feminine a genuine source of daily struggle for boys and men, its effects ripple far beyond their own particular lives. He points out that all manner of developmental psychologies converge on the view that same-sex friendships, especially among adolescent boys, serve as the primary laboratory for love beyond one's immediate family, specifically for heterosexual relationships and marriage: "Most schools of psychology agree that if we have not mastered these intimacy skills with someone of our own gender, we are not equipped truly to love someone of the opposite gender" (Culbertson 1996, 170).

*New York Times* columnist Maureen Dowd (2008) confirms this view in telling of a lecture titled "Whom Not to Marry" that Father Pat Conner, a seventy-nine-year-old Catholic priest from Bordentown, New Jersey, has been giving to high school seniors ("mostly girls because they're more interested") for the past forty years. When Dowd asked him to summarize his talk, Conner began by saying, "Never marry a man who has no friends. This usually means that he will be incapable of the intimacy that marriage demands. I am always amazed at the number of men I have counseled who have no friends. Since, as the Hebrew Scriptures say, 'Iron shapes iron and friend shapes friend,' what are his friends like?" (A10). When men fail to learn the lessons of love in intimate friendships with other men but still want to spend time with them, they tend to draw in and use women, and particularly their marital status, to prove their masculinity. Women become triangulated, serving as shields to protect men from anxiety generated by their homosocial desire.

But even adolescent boys without recourse to marriage rely on girls and women for this kind of cover. One artful expression of this dynamic among boys is director Alfonso Cuarón's (2001) *Y Tu Mamá También*, an evocative and funny, but ultimately sobering and melancholic, coming-of-age film set in his native Mexico. Its adolescent protagonists, Tenoch (Diego Luna) and Julio (Gael García Bernal), best friends since childhood, are surprised when Luisa (Maribel Verdú), the beautiful and mysterious estranged wife of Tenoch's older cousin, accepts the boys' invitation to join them on a spontaneous road trip to a nonexistent beach paradise. But the boys' friendship is shaken along the way as Luisa eventually sleeps with Tenoch, an act that evokes vitriolic jealously in Julio, who reacts by revealing a time when he severely betrayed his friend. When later Luisa seduces Julio in kind, the tension further escalates between the boys. More telling, however, is what reviewer Steve Vineberg (2002) calls "an unfamiliar intensity" that comes to the boys' relationship as Luisa, "so fed up with their feuding that she threatens to leave," compels them to make up. When they do, guided by "Luisa's sexual radar [that] identifies their own unacknowledged feelings about each other," the boys allow themselves to stumble, to their later revulsion, into an erotic mutual embrace that propels them far more than had any previous sexual encounters with their girlfriends or with Luisa into "the uncharted territory of adulthood" (37). As Luisa steps back, in other words, the boys become vulnerable to a previously unrecognized depth of desire between them.

In a very different kind of coming-of-age film, this one a crude Hollywood comedy, a teenage boy defends himself from the self-conscious aftermath of an unexpected moment of tenderness with his best friend by invoking the body of his friend's mother. His remark is another, less subtle, example of what Culbertson would recognize as a male form of hiding behind women to assuage homosocial anxiety. Near the end of producer Judd Apatow's (2007) *Superbad*, Seth (Jonah Hill) and Evan (Michael Cera), boyhood friends about to depart for different colleges, find themselves exhausted and relieved to have escaped the cops who broke up another friend's party.

Sprawled out for the night in sleeping bags on the floor of Evan's basement family room, their inhibitions lowered by alcohol, the boys reveal anxieties about their imminent separation and, with increasing revelry, the depths of their affection.

For the first time in their long friendship they hear each other saying again and again variations on the words *I love you, man*. Then just before drifting off to sleep Seth tweaks Evan's nose and says, "Boop, boop, boop. . . . Come here. Come here." The boys eke out an embrace despite the intervening sleeping bags. The scene ends as Seth says one last time, "I love you."

The next morning, the sun streaming in through the basement windows, first Seth, then Evan, wakes up. Now sober but remembering with disbelief the previous night's expressions of affection, they flounder in stilted conversation until Seth finally reasserts previous relational boundaries by an appeal to Evan's mother:

**Seth** *(to himself)*: What the fuck? (Evan wakes up). What up?

**Evan** *(hesitant)*: Morning . . . morning.

**Seth** *(anxious)*: I should get moving. I should get moving. I should be getting a move on, for sure.

**Evan** *(rescuing him)*: You don't . . . I mean, you don't have to, you know. I don't really have anything . . . going on. You don't have to rush off like that.

**Seth** *(awkward pause)*: You wanna hang out? I was, uh, gonna go to the mall.

**Evan** *(still nervous)*: I have to get, uh, a new comforter . . . for college. The mall . . . would sell that.

**Seth**: Cool. . . . So, uh, your mom's got huge tits.

At the far reaches of their conscious experience, young men like Tenoch and Julio, and Seth and Evan, are coming to sense that being a "man's man," as literary critic Eve Kosofsky Sedgwick points out, "is separated only by an invisible, carefully blurred, always-already-crossed line from being 'interested in men'" (Culbertson 1996, 160, quoting Sedgwick 1985, 89). Culbertson's project, by turns, focuses on ways that the Christian church has overcompensated for the threat posed by having to straddle this invisible line. He concludes that "until men can learn to form intimate friendships with other men in a manner which does not use women as a proof of their masculinity, the line between friendship and women-bartering homosociality will remain destructively blurred" (161).

Culbertson rightly stops short of suggesting any easy cure for these tensions and tendencies, which are reminiscent of what Freud identified as castration anxiety. Because, however, Culbertson sees homosocial anxiety more as a product of social conditioning than as biological bedrock, he appears to hold out more hope than Freud that older boys and adult men could somehow learn to move beyond their reflexive repudiation of the feminine. For Culbertson, the primary, perhaps the only, way for them to begin to repudiate this repudiation would be to come first to recognize, then to resist, the many cultural, especially religious, conventions that conspire to deny them intimate same-sex friendships. They first need to reclaim a sense of the importance of friendship as a laboratory of love. As we shall see, however, Culbertson underscores that boys' and men's prospects for doing so have been gravely compromised by centuries of church history and teaching.

## ONE SOUL IN TWO BODIES

Culbertson (1996) begins his essay on friendship by tracing the high regard for same-sex male friendships held by early shapers of the Christian theological tradition. Even as it was de rigueur for classical Greek and Roman writers to address the topic of friendship between men, so also did patristic theologians produce "derivative essays on friendship between men as the highest expression of God's love acted out in public" (151). Early Christian writers saw friends as gifts from God, evident in the claim, for example, that God directs "specific people's paths to cross in life so that they might have the opportunity to develop an intimate friendship" (155). Loyalty to these God-given friends, in turn, became of paramount importance to the patristic writers, expressed by some in expectations that a friend would turn "down opportunities for professional advancement in order to stay in the same location as one's best friend" and even, when possible, live under the same roof in order to maximize "intimacy through . . . shared daily contact" (157).

As an example of one such celebrated friendship, Culbertson focuses on the fourth-century friendship between Basil, the eventual bishop of Caesarea, and Gregory of Nazianzus, who became patriarch of Constantinople. "In their younger years," he writes,

> Gregory and Basil lived together as intimate roommates, shared everything, and each considered himself the alter ego of the other. In Epistle 58, Gregory writes to Basil, "The greatest benefit which life has brought me is your friendship and my intimacy with you." In Epistle 53, Gregory cries out that he has always loved Basil more than himself. In his oration at Basil's funeral, Gregory expresses his sense of being but half-alive, cut in two, haunted by thoughts of his dead friend. (157)

Culbertson explores how this passionate embrace between Basil and Gregory mirrored understandings of male friendship of Greek and Roman writers in late antiquity. He identifies three classical proverbs on friendship found "again and again in patristic literature, as though these proverbs were divinely inspired extensions of the foundational principle to 'love one's neighbor as one's self'" (Lev. 19:18): first, *"friends are one soul in two bodies"*; second, *"a friend is a second self"*; and finally, *"friends hold all things in common"* (151).

In placing high value on same-gender friendships, Culbertson says, the classical and patristic writers anticipated by centuries the claim of developmental psychologists, namely, "that homosocial love must not only precede heterosexual love, but must continue alongside it, in order for heterosexual love to survive. . . . Without [this] school of love, society would have no hope for the future" (170).

## TROUBLE IN THE SCHOOL OF LOVE

But trouble was brewing even from the outset in the early Christian school of homosocial love. Tensions were evident on a number of fronts, including, as hinted at in the previous quotation, in the ways the patristic writers managed intimate same-gender friendships in relation to married life, as well as in debates on the relative merits of marriage versus celibacy (cf. Brown 1988/2008; Boyarin 1995; Martin 1999). Divergent understandings also surfaced, however, concerning the nature of same-sex friendship itself.

Culbertson (1996) finds this latter tension played out in the friendship of Basil and Gregory, who, as noted, lived together in their younger years and considered each an alter ego of the other. But "when Basil became bishop of Caesarea, he not only abandoned his friend for a distant city," Culbertson writes, "but he did not even draw his intimate Gregory into consideration of whether to accept the election. Essentially, Gregory never forgave Basil for having left him" (157–58). He wrote "vitriolicly [sic] of his betrayal, his loss, his incredulity at being so summarily dropped by Basil" (158).

Important for our purposes, Culbertson sees this crisis between friends as stemming from competing philosophies about the evolution of friendships over time, with Basil representing Plato's approach and Gregory reflecting Aristotle's. "At question," Culbertson writes, "is whether friendship should move from particular to universal, or universal to particular" (158). He quotes Gilbert Meilaender:

> For Plato, friendship is a universal love which grows out of more particular, affective attachments. For Aristotle . . . , it is a narrowing down of the many toward whom we have good will to a few friends whom we especially choose. Plato's theory begins with a particular attachment, which then grows toward a more universal love. Aristotle's moves in precisely the opposite direction. (Meilaender 1981, in Culbertson 1996, 158)

Culbertson cites Basil's "Aescetic Sermon I" on Matthew 5:45, where Basil claims that "perfect love must be impartial in its imitation of God's love for humanity." By contrast, Gregory valued Basil not as a stepping stone to universal love but as a unique and matchless individual, and he valued their friendship precisely for its glorious partiality. Though Culbertson makes clear he favors Gregory's priority of the particular in the sphere of love, Christian orthodoxy over time instead elevated Basil's loftier perspective.

A lingering consequence of this spiritualizing tendency even today, Culbertson maintains, is that boys and men learn to dissociate their friendships from their bodies. Whereas some patristic writers emphasized the very physical nature of friendship, including living together under one roof, the eventual triumph of a Christian dualism that elevated the soul at the expense of the body led to suspicions if a man expressed appreciation for the physical body of his friend. When Augustine, for example, adopting Plato's trajectory from particular to universal love, conceives of friendship as "a Christian responsibility to be extended to all," the particularities of a friend's body—and, by extension, of one's own body—become peripheral, such that "almost anyone becomes loveable, just as God's love knows no partiality." Or as Adam Phillips (1995) puts it, "Finding ways of not being bodies . . . is integral to both Platonism and Christianity" (94). "Once friendship was spiritualized," Culbertson writes, "it was easily universalized; once universalized, it was essentially emasculated" (165). One finds, then, a kind of tragic irony in what amounts to a theologically legitimized disembodying—one could even say castration—of Christian boys and men. They are urged to renounce the embodied physicality of actual same-sex friendships as a surer path to spiritual manhood, emasculated in this way in order to attain true masculinity.

Culbertson finds the church's fingerprints everywhere apparent on the carnage wrought over centuries of this privileging of the universal in the Christian school of homosocial love. He points to recent studies in cultural anthropology, for example, which suggest that Christian missionaries of the eighteenth and nineteenth centuries appear to have spread homophobia as liberally as the gospel itself, over against a normative stance of "institutionalized bisexuality" evident in many pre-Christianized cultures, including those of Native Americans, the Hawaiians, and the Maori of New Zealand. He writes, "Defining homosexuality as either a crime or a sin is, then, at least culture-specific or ethnocentric, and is probably Christocentric" (163–64).

So too Culbertson discusses the so-called "Muscular Christianity" movement of the late nineteenth and early twentieth centuries and its resurgence in the Promise Keepers of the early 1990s (and per Worthen 2009, 20ff, continuing to resonate in certain influential evangelical churches today). In paying homage to the spiritual significance of an athletic male physique, these movements at first glance seem to defy Christian theology's traditional deference to the spirit. On closer inspection, however, Muscular Christianity's premise of the physical superiority of males and its push to expel all things effeminate from the church merely substituted (or perpetuated) a feminine/masculine dualism for a body/spirit dualism (Culbertson 168, quoting Jock Phillips 1987, 216). Repudiation of the feminine and its attendant anxieties are everywhere palpable in Muscular Christianity and its progeny. Culbertson writes, "The impact of Muscular Christianity was pervasive and international; a hundred years later, its residue continues to influence Christian suspicion of intimate male friendship," thereby further implicating Christianity in its instituting or, at least, its reinforcing what he rightly describes as "one of the most critical forms of oppression under which [boys and men] live" (168, 174).

## SUBVERSIVE QUALITIES OF MALE FRIENDSHIP

With these and other examples, Culbertson (1996) concludes that while patristic theology may have contributed to planting seeds of male homophobia, "it took the subsequent development of ecclesiastical power and authority for those seeds to overwhelm the positive evaluation of intimate male friendship as the highest expression of Christian love" (164).

He identifies three qualities of same-gender friendship that prove especially threatening to Christian orthodoxy in this regard. First, *"friendship is
by nature private."* Siding with the position of Gregory over Basil, Culbertson
believes that most boys and men are capable of maintaining, at most, only a
few close friendships. Whether because they are concerned that their same-
gender friendships will be greeted with suspicion by others or that their emotional resources quickly could become spread too thin, they tend to protect
their few friendships from "public scrutiny to avoid undue interference from
others." Whereas marriages, for most men, are quite public, close friendships
with other men are not; men put photographs of their wives and children, not
of their best friends, on their desks at work (171).

The private or antisocial nature of friendships means, second, that *"friendship is also anti-institutional."* Businesses, churches, and other institutions try
to regulate the friendships of their employees or constituents, Culbertson
observes, determining "who can be friends under what circumstances." Institutions recognize that friendships involve placing one's trust outside the institution, thereby potentially compromising the purposes and authority of the
corporate whole. "The institution loses its grip on its members when trust
is placed elsewhere," Culbertson writes, as when a man says, "'I'd rather be
spending my energies on my best friend than on furthering the power and
financial security of the company'" (171–72).

In a recent essay "A Theological Dictionary: F Is for Friendship," Martin
E. Marty (2009) lends support to Culbertson's claim that the threat for the
church in friendship centers on its private, anti-institutional nature. Marty
notes with some surprise that an entry for *friendship* does not "appear in the
score of English-language theological dictionaries" on his bookshelf, which
instead tend to skip from *Freud and theology* to *fundamentalism.* And this despite
the fact that friendship, he says,

> cannot be excluded from *biblical* dictionaries. Both the Hebrew and
> Greek words for friendship appear in the texts. Moses is called a friend
> of God, and friendship is modeled in the relationships of Naomi and
> Ruth and David and Jonathan. Perhaps most significantly, in John
> 15:15 Jesus says, "I have called you friends, because I have made
> known to you everything that I have heard from my Father." (10)

Marty speculates that the neglect of friendship in distinguished theological dictionaries of the past century may reflect the widespread influence of
Anders Nygren's (1953) *Agape and Eros.* There, Nygren stressed how different is *agape*, a divine form of love, from *"eros* and its correlates, like *philia*," the
love of friends, which depend on human desire:

Nygren, in the company of Kierkegaard, argues that friendship has an essentially selfish nature. In friendship, one chooses whose company to keep in order to meet the needs or interests of the self. The act of choosing, as Nygren points out, is based in part on desire for the other. And friendship brings with it an almost unavoidable and ungodlike exclusivity. (10)

Marty attempts to counter Nygren's view by suggesting that *friendship* does indeed belong in our theological lexicon, both as a witness to the character and inner life of a Trinitarian God and as a model for human relationships. But even Marty pulls his punches at this point by cautioning that a theological focus on friendship must "not lead to a sentimentalizing of God," whereby God becomes reduced to "something palsy and chummy" at the expense of our attention to God's wrathful "dark side" (10). In ending on this more guarded note, Marty undercuts the radical nature of Christian friendship that his essay seeks to promote, thus inadvertently underscoring Culbertson's own claims about the historical suspicion of friendship in Christian theology.

Third and finally, and in addition to the private and anti-institutional nature of friendship, Culbertson maintains that *friendship is unproductive.* Unlike marriage, it tends not to contribute to producing children, maintaining attractive homes and neighborhoods, or generating tangible goods and services prized by the larger community (172). From the community's perspective, friendship tends not to be a terribly fruitful way for boys and men to spend their time.

Given the private, anti-institutional, and unproductive nature of same-gender friendships, those who seek out such friendships unintentionally threaten to subvert the authority and power of established institutions, including the church. Over against theological teachings that impose homosocial anxiety on boys and men, however, Culbertson presses for a liberating theology derived from among the earliest church fathers. Such a "patristic liberation theology" would encourage boys and men to subvert familiar humiliations at the hands of institutions they serve. By learning to befriend their bodies and embody their friendships, they would come to discover a reliable means of God's grace in the world.

## A PROBLEMATIC FIRST STEP

Culbertson's clinical and pastoral concern for the everyday struggles of boys and men leads him to incontrovertible evidence of Christianity's collusion in their emotional and physical isolation. By making friendship appear homosexually dangerous and thereby dissociating it from boys' and men's physical bodies, Christian theologies have fed on and exacerbated the funny emotions that males experience with one another. Policing themselves and one another in countless spoken and unspoken ways in Western (and other) Christianized cultures, boys learn early on to suppress even the faintest signs of homosocial interest, affection, or desire.

Adults, for their part, want boys to have close male friends but then worry when they actually do. As journalist Malina Saval (2009) points out in *The Secret Lives of Boys: Inside the Raw Emotional World of Male Teens*, a collection of case studies drawn from extensive interviews with a diverse group of ten adolescent boys over a period of several years, "we push boys to form meaningful, long-lasting friendships, and we want them to have confidants they can trust. But if they spend *too* much time with their male friends (and not enough with girls), then many of us leap to the conclusion that our sons must be gay." She quotes psychologist Niobe Way (Way & Chu 2004), coeditor of *Adolescent Boys: Exploring Diverse Cultures of Boyhood*:

> "The cultural definition in America of being gay is a guy having a close guy friend," proffers Way. . . . People, she says, often falsely assume that teenage boys are gay just because they have a close relationship with another boy. This can make it extremely difficult for male teens to foster such friendships without feeling that we are all questioning their sexual orientation, an uncommon scenario for adolescent boys who are just beginning to explore their waking sexuality. "It's paranoia," posits Way. "And this microcosm that occurs among boys and their parents reflects the macrocosmic existence of grown men." (91)

This kind of anxiety, of course, at once reflects and leads to what Culbertson describes as one of the most critical forms of male oppression and what Saval sees as "the ubiquitous loneliness pervading teenage boyhood culture today," a feeling expressed by every boy in her study: "'I don't know how I am going to fit into your book,' [fourteen-year-old] Maxwell professes with a long, weary sigh. 'It's tough to relate with other kids. Honestly, not to brag, but I don't know many kids like me'" (48). Saval concludes by suggesting, with only a hint of irony, that their sense of "not fitting in" with others their age is in fact what unites adolescent boys: "In their collective sense of not belonging . . . , they share a common bond" (240). They belong to the group of those who do not belong. Echoing Culbertson's own pleas, she writes.

> Boys need other boys . . . to talk with. They need at least one person in whom they are consistently able to confide. To keep boys grounded and sane, it's crucial that we encourage our young people

to forge trusting, enduring friendships with others, to show them that boys can be close friends without all the unhealthy and unnecessary assumptions about their sexuality. (154)

I applaud these kinds of calls for boys and men to stand against those who, under cloak of Christian morality or of cultural codes of manhood, would deprive them of the unrivaled intimacy afforded by same-gender friendships. Equally laudable are Culbertson's pragmatic efforts in other writings to instruct boys and men—in a respectful, step-by-step way—on how to initiate and develop close same-gender friendships while alerting them to potential hazards along the way (see Culbertson 1996, 173–74; and esp. 1994, 80–81).

It is worth noting, however, that first among the steps he suggests that boys and men should take in establishing a friendship is one of convincing themselves—or of being convinced—that committed, same-gender friendships are actually worth pursuing. In discussing this first step, Culbertson (1994) acknowledges that most boys and men will likely experience "some anxiety" in coming to this awareness and therefore should be encouraged to remind themselves over and over again "that there's nothing weird or effeminate about wanting a friend" (80). But for a first step, as both Saval's and Way's research with adolescent boys appears to confirm, Culbertson may be asking too much of boys and men in this. For many or even most of them it may be a deal breaker. If they were capable of accomplishing this first step—convincing themselves that there is nothing weird or effeminate about wanting a friend—they most likely would not have experienced friendship problems to begin with. For most boys and men, the very sense of wanting or needing a friend is precisely the problem. The desire for a friend, though oddly familiar at the far reaches of their conscious experience, *is* weird or effeminate to them, indeed the very *definition* of weird or effeminate. At those times when it washes into conscious awareness, it is felt as a threat to their sense of masculine self-sufficiency.

This is not to say that boys or men cannot or do not have friends, for of course they can and do. But as Culbertson himself makes clear in his suggested first step toward acquiring friends, in almost every instance it *feels unnatural*—that is, it goes against the grain and stirs up a good deal of anxiety—for them to have, or to *want* to have, friends. If boys and men were in a position to take this first step, they would have no need of taking it. So we find ourselves on the horns of a dilemma. Older adolescent boys find themselves caught between competing claims of sincere homosocial desire and rigidly monitored social prohibitions, a conflict likely reflected in Barbara J. Risman's observation, noted earlier, that they appear to be "frozen in time" (in Warner 2009).

To better understand the persistence of this paralysis from generation to generation of boys and men, it may be worthwhile to return again
for a moment to Freud's last and, according to his biographer Ernst Jones
(Leupold-Löwenthal 1987, 50), best technical paper on psychoanalysis. In
"Analysis Terminable and Interminable" (1937/1964), Freud finds himself
drawn to portray the anxiety that I suggest fuels the sense in older boys that
there is something "weird or effeminate" about wanting a friend as arising
from a universal bisexual constitution of persons.

## THE CONUNDRUM OF BISEXUALITY

Freud thought of bisexuality in many different ways over the course of his
professional life. As Marjorie Garber (2000) methodically explores in a chapter on Freud in her book *Bisexuality and the Eroticism of Everyday Life*, bisexuality variously meant for him "anything from (1) having two sets of sexual
organs to (2) having two psyches, one male and one female, to (3) having a
precarious and divided sexuality which is fluid rather than fixed with regard to
both identification and object" (203–4). The early Freud could use the coldly
clinical term "amphigenic inverts" to describe bisexual persons, making his
transformation by the time of "Analysis Terminable and Interminable" all
the more remarkable. There at the end of his life, he considered bisexuality
more simply as a capacity to have both male and female sexual partners and,
even more striking, as a universal given in human sexual life. Though my male
seminary students in their twenties still reflexively reject Freud's claim, finding it to be as radical (or laughable) today as it may have seemed to Freud's
original readers nearly a century ago, a biologically inevitable bisexuality constituted for him the very bedrock of the human soul—a bedrock, as noted,
that he became convinced was impenetrable by means of psychoanalysis. So
while it remained something of a mystery or conundrum for Freud even at
the end of his life, we find in his valedictory remarks on bisexuality at least a
flicker of hope for illuminating, if not fully overcoming, the impasse found
in the first step Culbertson instructs adolescent boys and men to take toward
forming same-gender friendships—that of telling themselves it is not weird
or effeminate to want a friend.

Freud published the essay that some scholars have called "a sort of scientific last will and testament" (Zimmerman and Bento Mostardiero 1987, 89;
cf. Fromm 1994, 15) at the age of eighty-one. In the fourteen years prior to
its publication, he had suffered a painful cancer of the jaw and thirty-three
surgeries on his mouth with little relief. The Nazi rampage was everywhere
apparent in Europe by 1937, with Freud's own books previously having been

burned in public bonfires by the Germans. One year after the publication of "Analysis," Austria would be annexed to Germany. Fearing especially for the life of his daughter Anna, Freud and his immediate family would flee his beloved Vienna for London, where he would live just over one year before his death in 1939.

Given this grim setting, it is no wonder that James Strachey, in his commentary on the *Standard Edition* (1926/1959) of Freud's works, acknowledges that in this essay the reader "cannot escape an impression of [Freud's] pessimism, particularly in regard to the therapeutic efficacy of psychoanalysis" (Leupold-Löwenthal 1987, 47–48). There is a sober realism here in Freud's claims for what psychoanalysis can and cannot do. An undercurrent running throughout the essay seems to be Freud's ongoing attempt to do battle against fundamentalisms on several fronts—against religious and Nazi fundamentalisms, to be sure, but also perhaps more courageously against psychoanalytic fundamentalism, whereby his colleagues might be inclined to claim more efficacy for psychoanalysis than even Freud himself would allow.

More significant even than his resistance to these, however, may be his choosing to conclude the essay with one last attempt in his lifetime to strike down a kind of sexual, particularly heterosexual, fundamentalism. The essay climaxes, so to speak, in a discussion of bisexuality. More specifically, it builds to its concluding claims for a ubiquitous, though usually repressed, bisexual bedrock of the human soul. He writes,

> It is well known that at all periods there have been, as there still are, people who can take as their sexual objects members of their own sex as well as of the opposite one, without the one trend interfering with the other. We call such people bisexuals, and we accept their existence without feeling much surprise about it. *We have come to learn, however, that every human being is bisexual in this sense and that his libido is distributed, either in a manifest or a latent fashion, over objects of both sexes.* But we are struck by the following point. Whereas in the first class of people the two trends have got on together without clashing, in the second and more numerous class they are in a state of irreconcilable conflict. A man's heterosexuality will not put up with any homosexuality, and *vice versa*. If the former is the stronger it succeeds in keeping the latter latent and forcing it away from satisfaction in reality. On the other hand, there is no greater danger for a man's heterosexual function than its being disturbed by his latent homosexuality. (Freud 1937/1964, 243–44, emphasis added)

This bisexual "danger" and the repudiation of the feminine to which it leads—or by which it gets expressed—go right to the heart of the funny emotions that boys and men experience around same-gender friendships. But for Freud, unlike for Culbertson, this danger cannot be willed away simply by a boy's or man's telling himself over and over again that it is not weird or effeminate to "want" (now in either sense of the word) a male friend. Though Freud would allow that this wound might be *curated*—scrupulously tended, dressed, and kept from infection—he would not, in his lifetime, concede that it could ever be *cured*. In this we find a plausible explanation for the so-called time warp in which boys perpetually live. Their sense of danger is impenetrable. It is bedrock.

Marjorie Garber says that in his earlier book *Civilization and Its Discontents*, Freud (1930/1961) claimed that "repression *grounds* civilization" and "treats sexual dissidents as if they were a subject population capable of revolt" (Garber 2000, 204–5). By means of repression, civilization colonizes sexuality, especially so-called deviant sexual expression. Garber writes,

> If repression grounds civilization, it is bisexuality, in its many guises, that is being repressed. Repressed for our own good. Bisexuality is that upon the repression of which society depends for its laws, codes, boundaries, social organization—everything that defines "civilization" as we know it. (206)

Seven years later, in "Analysis Terminable and Interminable," Freud underscores again that, however necessary to a degree for upholding the institutions of society, including religious ones, such repression—specifically the repression of bisexuality—is also in essence always a falsification, a form of self-deception, a sacrifice of truth (Freud 1937/1964, 235).

In the way of such sacrifices, it comes at great cost. The highest of these costs, Freud says, is the repudiation of the feminine, one of the clearest expressions of which for older boys, I am suggesting, is the increasing likelihood of their forfeiting intimate friendships with other boys. Though it remains a costly psychological falsification or distortion, the act of living *with* the inner conflict generated by denying their ambisexuality becomes preferable to living *free from* such conflict. Psychosocial conflict around castration anxiety, the repudiation of the feminine, or what more commonly today gets expressed as homophobia becomes the more familiar, even preferred experience for older adolescent boys and men. Rather than simply act on their bisexual desires, boys and men almost invariably choose to live in vaguely conscious conflict over them. In something of a strange twist, then, Freud concludes in "Analysis" that a boy's or man's denial (or, more accurately, his repression) of his bisexual constitution is, or becomes over time, a form of masochism or self-hatred. Masochism becomes a normative sexual experience for boys and men, a stand-in for bisexual desire, which is, for its part, renounced as a perversion (Freud 1937/1964, 242–44). Sex without self-hatred, that is, sex without refusing an important aspect of their own self-experience, becomes as unimaginable for boys and men as sex with another male or even intimate same-sex friendship.

## THE FORBIDDEN COMPLEXITY
## OF BOYHOOD DESIRE

What accounts for this strange state of affairs? What links male homophobia and a boy's struggle with close same-sex friendships to an original childhood bisexuality? In his recent book *Going Sane: Maps of Happiness*, Adam Phillips (2005) offers a straightforward clue by declaring that the most truly sane persons among us recognize that "everyone is bisexual because everyone has had a mother and father (absent and/or present) who they have loved and desired and hated" (197–98). Bisexuality originates, in Freud's understanding, in a child's early love and desire for *both* mother and father. But navigating the dynamics of these two loves soon grows complex for the child.

In several recent books, Donald Capps (1997, 2002; and Dykstra, Cole, and Capps, 2007) traces in meticulous detail the complexities of Freud's arguments for these connections, especially as they affect a boy's spiritual quest and lead to a religious form of male melancholy. Capps (1997) draws especially on Freud's essay "Mourning and Melancholia" (1917/1963) to develop his case for a uniquely male approach to spirituality, where religion comes to serve as a balm of sorts for boys between the ages of three and five who mourn the loss of their mothers:

> As Freud makes clear in his famous essay . . . , the core issue in melancholia is that the sufferer has a "plaint" against another, that is, the lost object. Rightly or wrongly, legitimately or not, the sufferer blames his mother for his plight or, if he finds it too threatening to cast blame on her, he internalizes the blame in the form of *self-*reproach. Melancholiacs, then, are people who cannot bring themselves to blame directly the one against whom they have a grievance but instead internalize the object of blame and punish that aspect of self with which the object is now identified. (6–7)

The arena in which boys "seek what they lost in their relationships with their mothers," Capps says, is religion, though usually not religion in the conventional sense (7). Instead, they are more likely to adopt what Capps calls either a *religion of honor* whereby the boy develops an especially vigilant or hypermoral conscientiousness to try to win back his mother's affection by becoming an honorable, well-behaved boy; or a *religion of hope*, whereby the boy, thrust now into a larger world as a result of the separation, begins a quest for objects that resemble the one he has lost. Boys typically express their religious yearnings through all manner of honorable service and a perpetual pilgrimage of searching and hope (Capps 2002, 45–52; Dykstra, Cole, and Capps 2007, 133–38).

Capps recognizes the authentic merits of these unconventional and distinctly male forms of religious expression. But since the religions of honor and hope function to hold in check the rage and sadness the boy otherwise would have directed toward his mother in response to the original loss, they contribute to his turning that rage and sadness inward. Rather than appropriately mourning the original mother loss for which he holds no blame, he instead develops a melancholic religious disposition susceptible to excessive self-reproach.

In an ideal world, some of this self-directed rage and sadness stemming from the boy's loss of the intense bond with his mother in the oedipal years would be mitigated by an increasing identification and deepening bond with his father. This ideal, however, is never fully realized. Instead, while it is common and culturally sacrosanct for boys to end up *identifying* with their fathers, it is unusual and culturally suspect for boys to *bond* with them. To identify with one's father is to desire to be *like* him, a desire culturally and religiously sanctioned. To bond with one's father, on the other hand, is to desire to *have* him, even in a sexual sense, and this, of course, is culturally and religiously prohibited. A five-year-old boy unconsciously attempting to console himself for the oedipal loss of his mother, Capps points out, knows enough to grasp that being a man involves being like his father but certainly not emotionally or physically *possessing* him. However much the boy longs for both, identification and bonding with his father are in fact mutually incompatible in the real world (Capps 2002, 66–77).

Thus, a young boy's bisexual interests only compound the sadness and rage of his oedipal losses, given that he holds intense emotional and physical desires not just for his mother but for his father. Religion becomes a consolation prize (for it actually can and sometimes does console), a salve of sorts in response to castration anxiety that allows boys perhaps the only acceptable way to love another male, specifically a male God. But because religion colludes in the repression of boys' complex sexual desires, it becomes an outlet that, however soothing, exacts from them a certain price.

Capps recognizes the high price that boys pay for their religious devotion to a Father God as an emerging and enduring *homophobia*, the inevitable consequence of a boy's fated repression of his desire for his father. Because he chooses to identify with his father as a man rather than to bond with him as a son, subsequent same-sex relationships stir again and again in the boy his original but relinquished object choice of the father (Capps 2002, 81–83). This calls to mind Culbertson's earlier observation that "fear of unexpected arousal" is the primary form of homosocial anxiety in boys and men.

One result of all this, as James Baldwin (1985/2001) laments near the end of his life in an essay on masculine desire, is that the originally more complex sexual interests of boys and men become sorted instead into familiar but psychologically costly binary oppositions:

> The American *ideal*, then, of sexuality appears to be rooted in the American ideal of masculinity. This ideal created cowboys and Indians, good guys and bad guys, punks and studs, tough guys and softies, butch and faggot, black and white. It is an ideal so paralytically infantile that it is virtually forbidden—an unpatriotic act—that the American boy evolve into the complexity of manhood. (208)

The relational detritus of this sexual simplification is everywhere apparent in psyche, church, and culture, leading Baldwin to observe—and Freud, Culbertson, and Capps may well be inclined to concur—"that the male desire for a male roams everywhere, avid, desperate, unimaginably lonely, culminating often in drugs, piety, madness, or death" (Baldwin 1985/2001, 212).

If at the distant edges of consciousness older adolescent boys begin to sense, with Baldwin, some nascent longing for another world of male companionship, most could not imagine being in a position to actually express it. The odds of boys and young men coming to acknowledge that at some level they are inherently bisexual would seem to be less even than those of convincing themselves it is "not weird or effeminate" to want male friends. It seems strange for me to say this, given what I teach for a living and what I explore in these chapters, but I am beginning to wonder whether curators of funny emotions would do well instead simply to honor the need for adolescent boys and young men to keep silent about the uncomfortable truths of their lives—maybe not forever silent but at least for a time, possibly a long time, and even among those they know best of all. Yes, as they draw nearer to adulthood, adolescent boys actually do long for another world of male intimacy. But in *this* world, the so-called *real* world, there is no uncomplicated (or patriotic) way for them to say so. Bedrock is bedrock, or so, at least, it seems.

This does not mean, however, that a curator of their funny emotions lacks any resources or plays no role in the lives of older adolescent boys and young men. To the contrary, while one would be wise not to expect to *cure* them fully of the inevitable simplifications of homophobia and its ramifications for their friendships, we will consider in the following chapter several constructive functions of the curator for attending to their disconcerting emotions and deep gossip. Understanding the positive value of these functions, whether fulfilled by boys themselves in friendships with one another or by adults who care for them, will make for wise and faithful companions on the spiritual journeys of adolescent boys.

# 4

# Friendly Fire

---

**friend·ly fire**, *n. (military)* firing by one's own side, especially
when it harms one's own personnel; shots fired at one accidentally
by soldiers from one's own army

In the previous chapter, we considered how same-sex friendships become
increasingly prone to anxiety as boys move from adolescence into young
adulthood, leading Philip L. Culbertson to claim that "men's fear of intimate
male friendship is one of the most critical forms of oppression under which
they live" (1996, 174). Culbertson rightly attributes much responsibility for
this state of affairs to Christian theology's historic emphasis on the spiritual
over the earthly and the universal over the particular in the sphere of human
love. But we also saw how Freud's long struggle to understand the intractable
nature of the repudiation of the feminine makes for a sobering countervalence
to Culbertson's prescription for those boys and men who wish to resist its
tyranny, namely, that they begin by assuring themselves that there is nothing
weird or effeminate about wanting male friends. Freud is less encouraging
about such prospects than is Culbertson, seeing the problem as a direct consequence of their bisexual origins and constitution.

I find much of value in both of these perspectives. Culbertson's indictment
of the Christian church in promoting homosocial anxiety is at once convincing
and convicting. As a fellow pastoral theologian and counselor, I identify with
his desire to find pragmatic ways to counter its isolating effects in the lives of
actual boys and men. But equally compelling is Freud's somber assessment
of how psychologically entrenched and ubiquitous is this repudiation of the
feminine among boys and men. His views lead me to believe that, whatever

71

strides individual boys and men may make to limit its impact on their own lives and friendships, a collective sense of remaining frozen in a time warp of vigilant masculinity will shadow them down through the generations.

This means that while it may be difficult to envision long-term *cures* for the funny emotions that increasingly accompany their same-sex friendships as boys mature into adult men, there are ways that adults who care for them and that peers who actually befriend them can and do become, in effect, *curators* of their funny emotions, those who offer modest care more than miraculous cure. With a judicious style and an ear attuned for deep gossip, the curator of funny emotions becomes a redemptive companion on the spiritual journeys of older adolescent boys.

In this chapter, we consider three constructive functions of the curator, all drawn from the Latin root *humus*, meaning "of the soil or earth," for attending to young men's disconcerting feelings and deep gossip. Why *humus*? If, as Culbertson claims, the early church disembodied or emasculated friendships among men by universalizing and elevating them to the heavenly heights, it may be of help especially to Christian boys and young men today to revisit Gospel texts and precepts that encourage them in navigating the uncomfortable realities of actual friendships much closer to the earthly depths. Ultimately, I pursue a portrait of Jesus as curator of funny emotions, one who finds the essence of the spiritual life in those ways, however halting and impious, that adolescent boys and young men already *can* and *do*, in fact, relate to and care for one another.

Specifically, the down-to-earth curator of funny emotions would do anything possible, first and foremost, to thwart the *humiliation* of boys and men. He or she would attend to and honor, second, the nuances of male *humor* as an inoculation of sorts against humiliation and as among the surest expressions of young men's deep gossip. Finally, such a curator would enlist a more *humble, human*, and *humane Jesus* to fortify any private, unproductive, same-sex friendships boys and men do manage to eke out over against the demands for good corporate citizenship that prevail everywhere around and within them. In these functions and more, a curator offers generous care and a common ear for emotions too funny finally to cure and gossip too deep fully to convey.

## PREVENTING HUMILIATION
## AROUND FUNNY EMOTIONS

Adam Phillips (2005) ends his book on the nature of sanity by saying that it would be sane to take

> for granted that everyone is even more confused than they seem. Havoc is always wreaked in fast cures for confusion. The sane believe

that confusion, acknowledged, is a virtue; and that *humiliating another person is the worst thing we ever do*. Sanity should not be our word for the alternative to madness; it should refer to *whatever resources we have to prevent humiliation*. (199, emphasis added)

Because "everyone is even more confused than they seem," curators of funny emotions, more than anything else, would do everything in their power *to avoid humiliating others*, to avoid pointing out their confusion or confusing them further. This at times may involve letting boys and young men keep their secrets, even from themselves.

I learned this lesson the hard way recently in one of my seminary courses. The class was large, about seventy-five students, and at one point in one particular class session—I can't even remember now what we were discussing at the time—I made the mistake of veering off script and mentioned in passing something of what I discussed in the previous chapter, namely, that I think everyone is bisexual *in some sense*. An audible, if not quite collective, gasp arose from the class. I had long believed—or, at least, had long wrestled with—the thoughts conveyed by the words that slipped out that day, but in more than a dozen previous years of teaching I had never spoken them quite so directly. The students' reaction alerted me instantly to the fact that I had entered dangerous territory, and I knew they would have a lot more to say outside my hearing around the lunch tables in the cafeteria after class. After finding myself somewhat unsettled by their response, I tried to add a bit more nuance to what I had said, telling them that despite being somehow originally bisexual, over time most people—or most men, anyway (cf. Diamond 2008)—develop a relatively clear and persistent sense of sexual orientation. But many of the students just did not seem to be buying it.

Then, however, another interesting thing happened. Gregory Ellison, my teaching assistant in the course, spoke up. He reminded the class of his field work at the time as a counselor in a program in inner-city Newark designed to help African American young men between the ages of fifteen and twenty-four in transitioning from prison to the outside world. Greg and another recent Princeton Seminary graduate, Torry Winn, were responsible for initiating tough and honest conversations as coleaders of support groups for these men for six or so weeks prior to their final release from incarceration.

In response to the class's reaction to my comment about an inherent bisexuality, Greg told the students that he and Torry consistently felt sexual tension in the room during their group sessions with these young men, all with massive muscles shaped by prison-yard workouts and all known on the streets of their respective communities as the toughest of men. But in the group sessions in this world apart, Greg said, these hypermasculine young men showed no qualms about sitting close to each other, men on the floor sitting between the legs of men on the sofas, touching each other, putting their arms around each other's shoulders, and playing with each other's hair. They somehow felt free in that setting to demonstrate what struck Greg and Torry as remarkable expressions of intimacy that these same men would never be allowed— or allow themselves—on the street. Eventually, Greg and Torry found the words to acknowledge to each other that what they sensed were not ordinary expressions of affection among the young men in the room but instead a palpable sexual tension, and both coleaders thought that they themselves were handling it without undue alarm. But Greg also told our students that *there was no way he and Torry could point out to the men in their care what they were witnessing and feeling*, for even to raise the subject would be to bring all such expressions of intimacy to an abrupt and decisive end.

I was relieved that Greg shared this story with my class, for it seemed to carry a lot of weight with the students. This may have been less because it was a timely example of what I had been trying to say, although it was, and more because the hypermasculine qualities of the young men he described so fully compensated, in some students' minds, for their expressions of mutual intimacy (in the way that male athletes are permitted physical expressions of affection with teammates). But Greg and Torry's expressed inability to say to the young men in their care what in fact as curators they had witnessed and discussed among themselves also reminded me that effective caregiving does not mean having to say everything one notices, thinks, or feels in the relationship, especially with older adolescent boys and young men. To say aloud what one notices as a counselor or caregiver at times may be a disservice to those one is trying to assist.

Greg and Torry, certainly first by discerning and attending to expressions of ambisexual intimacy in friendships among hypermasculine young men, but then, as important, *by not speaking what they noticed to those same men*, were functioning as powerful curators of their funny emotions. Curators *notice, nurture, and uphold*, but may be wise *not to necessarily point out*, what Ginsberg and Abelove (2003) might recognize as the *deep gossip* of these young men's lives. At some level close to the surface of conscious experience, these young men knew something about themselves—about their homosocial or ambisexual interests—that could not be expressed or exposed verbally but that distinguished them from male peers in less sobering social circumstances. Recall that deep gossip, according to Abelove, is "illicit . . . information [that is] an indispensable resource for those who are in any sense or measure disempowered, as those who experience funny emotions may be"—a form of self-expression that "circulates in subterranean ways and *touches on matters hard to grasp* and of crucial concern." In the safety of their group sessions, it is possible that the deep gossip of the incarcerated young men facing the anxiety of imminent release from prison was being expressed in the form of their *actual* touching and tender grasping (Abelove 2003, xii, emphasis added). Preventing humiliation, sometimes by not speaking what one knows, is the first rule of thumb for curators of the funny emotions of boys and men.

I clipped and filed away a newspaper essay titled "Iron Bonding" that impressed me at the height of the men's movement of the early 1990s. Its author, Alan Buczynski (1992), was a hard-hat urban ironworker with a college degree in English who at that time was dating a graduate student in English literature. He said that as a result of living in these two very different social worlds, he "bounced between blue-collar maulers and precise academicians. My conversations range from fishing to Foucault, derricks to deconstruction." At a dinner party, a friend of his girlfriend asked him whether the men he worked with on the cranes ever said, "I love you" to each other. He writes, "I replied, 'Certainly. All the time.' I am still dissatisfied with this answer. Not because it was a lie, but because it was perceived as one." He explains:

> Ironworkers are otherwise very direct, yet when emotional issues arise we speak to one another in allegory and parable. One of my co-workers, Cliff, is a good story-teller, with an understated delivery: "The old man got home one night, drunk, real messed up and got to roughhousing with the cat. Old Smoke, well she laid into him, scratched him good. Out comes the shotgun. The old man loads up, chases Smoke into the front yard and blam! Off goes the gun. My Mom and my sisters and me we're all screamin'. Smoke comes walkin' in the side door. Seems the old man blew away the wrong cat, the neighbor's Siamese. Red lights were flashin' against the house, fur was splattered all over the lawn, the cops cuffed my old man and he's hollerin' and man, I'll tell you, I was cryin'." (MM12)

Commenting on Cliff's story, Buczynski says,

> Now, we didn't all get up from our beers and go over and hug him. This was a story, not therapy. Cliff is amiable, but tough, more inclined to solving any perceived injustices with his fists than verbal banter, but I don't need to see him cry to know that he can. He has before, and he can tell a story about it without shame, without any disclaimers about being "just a kid," and that's enough for me. (MM12)

Allegory and parable to express the deepest emotional truths; stories, not therapy; not needing to see a man cry to know that he can: these strike me as assorted means by which boys and men go about expressing their deep gossip.

Donald Capps (1997) likewise touches on the value of emotional indirec-
tion among men in his preface to *Men, Religion, and Melancholia*, a book he
dedicated to his son John. He writes,

> I have profited from many personal conversations in recent years with
> students and colleagues on the topic of this book, but those that espe-
> cially stand out in my mind are ones I had with John Capps, who
> sensed by the rather serious tone of our conversations that the topic
> of melancholy has for me a personal subtext, *which mercifully remained,
> for the most part, unspoken but understood.* (xii–xiii, emphasis added)

Capps's gratitude for his son's reticence to ask the obvious question underscores that a curator of funny emotions—those ubiquitous but forbidden
desires for male bonding that lead in boys and men to impenetrable isolation,
religious melancholy, masochistic self-loathing, or what Baldwin (1985/2001)
describes as "drugs, piety, madness, or death" (212)—would go to great
lengths to prevent humiliating a father, son, mentor, protégé, or friend. This
includes, if need be, leaving some important questions unasked, some crucial
matters unspoken but understood.

## HUMOR AS INOCULATION AGAINST HUMILIATION

A second observation for curators of funny emotions, also drawing on the
root *humus*, is that funny emotions are *funny* in two senses of the word. I have
focused thus far on the second of Abelove's two meanings of *funny*, namely,
the kind of emotions *likely to be made fun of*—those found to be humiliating or
shameful and therefore mocked, derided, or stigmatized in church or culture.
But Abelove also noted in passing that emotions are funny in another sense,
that is, when "they are associated with fun or pleasure." There is a *ha-ha*
funny as well as a *peculiar* funny, and the former, more usual sense is also
worth retaining here as we consider becoming curators of the funny emotions
of adolescent boys and young men. Sometimes funny emotions, however dis-
tressing, also prove to be laugh-out-loud funny, as in Buczynski's account of
Cliff's story of his father blowing away the wrong cat. The deep, subterranean gossip of adolescent boys and young men is often, perhaps most often,
found in their humor (see Capps, 2002, 2005b; and Dykstra, Cole, and Capps,
2007). This is even more likely to be the case when the funny emotions boys
are trying to express have to do with their physical bodies and sexual, especially ambisexual, interests.

Culbertson is troubled, remember, by church teachings that in effect
emasculate boys and men by spiritualizing and universalizing the nature of

friendship. By elevating Basil's idealized notion that "perfect love must be impartial in its imitation of God's love for humanity," that is, that Christians need to love all humanity at the expense of loving anyone in particular, the church inadvertently encouraged boys and young men to dissociate friendships from their physical bodies. Their bodies instead remain for them under wraps, undercover, underground, subterranean. In light of this masculine reality, then, humor becomes for them a royal road back to the body. Humor is one way, perhaps the most common way, they gossip about forbidden interests and unpatriotic desires.

In Oscar Hijuelos's (2008) young-adult novel *Dark Dude*, as one example, two teenage Latino boys from inner-city New York are planning to run away from home, for good reason, to live with a friend on a farm in Wisconsin. As they prepare to flee the city, one of the boys, Jimmy, rifles through the protagonist Rico's overloaded duffle bag to rid it of excess stuff. Hijuelos writes in Rico's voice,

> Then [Jimmy] picked out a magnifying glass.
> And unless you're planning to jerk off *a lot* out there," he said to me, "and I know you probably *are*, we can ditch this magnifying glass, right?"
> And he put that aside.
> "Har, har," I said. "Very funny." (132–33)

Boys and men joke like this all the time, and such humor conveys, in a subterranean way, matters hard to grasp and of crucial concern. In this case, these matters include, among other things, bisexual anxiety or seduction, insecurities around penis size, and an implicit permission to masturbate, even frequently.

That such ordinary expressions of humor, especially sexually charged humor, have anything to do with, and are likely among the most important signifiers of, the spiritual interests of adolescent boys may come at first as something of a surprise. But how else could they talk with as much safety or deniability about these intimate, therefore spiritual, concerns?

As often as not, these spiritual interests and concerns center on their genitals. Indeed, why would they not, given even biblical precedents (Gen. 17:9-14) that, as one instructive example, locate the sign of the divine covenant precisely there?[1] A similar but much more current link can be found in director Judd Apatow's (2009) *Funny People*, a film about a famous, middle-aged stand-up comedian (played by Adam Sandler) diagnosed with an incurable cancer. The film includes comedy-club routines, and when pressed by a reporter on the seeming incongruity between the film's somber wrestling with the harsh dictates of a sudden confrontation with death and its unending stream of penis jokes, Apatow makes clear that this juxtaposition did not occur by chance. Rather, it was inevitable, he says, given his challenge to press the film's target audience of twenty-something young men to reflect on their mortality:

> "I wanted to accurately portray how comedians speak to each other," [Apatow] says. "The vast majority of their conversations are about their penises and testicles and size and what they might do to them and what they hope someone else does to them. We debated it a lot. We said, 'There are a lot of jokes in the crotch area.' Then we started thinking about our friends, and someone said, 'I think this is still about 10% of what most of our comic friends are doing in a 24-hour period,' and that's the funny thing." (Wloszczyna 2009, D1–2)

Humor, for Apatow, is serious business. His artistic intuitions lead him to make what seems for older boys and young men a completely organic but ordinarily unrecognized connection between irreverent humor and their most urgent spiritual concerns.

But would not this second principle for curators of funny emotions—that of attending to and respecting the hidden messages and positive functions of male humor, especially humor around sexuality and the body—work against the first principle of protecting another at all costs from humiliation? Isn't Jimmy's locker-room humor precisely intended to humiliate Rico?

Not exactly, and it is unlikely that Rico would take it that way. Instead, Jimmy's quip about the magnifying glass and "jerking off" serves as a redemptive—because embodied—kind of subterranean communication about matters difficult to talk about, as a kind of iron bonding between boys.

Why? Adam Phillips (2002) devotes a good portion of his essay "On Being Laughed At" to discussing ways that humor can be used destructively to humiliate others. Humor can stifle free expression, harden or intensify even minor differences between persons or groups, and become the enemy of sociability and even democracy. But it is also the case, Phillips maintains, that mild humor used carefully among friends has the positive therapeutic effect of "generously diminishing us; it lowers us down gently from our own ideals. It exposes our wish for exposure" (37). Unlike destructive humor that mortifies its victim by concentrating a shaming Klieg light of unwanted exposure on the self, gentler forms of ridicule such as teasing among friends allow for "the pleasure of yielding, of abrogating one's self-protective images" (41; cf. also Keltner 2008, 2009). Since *yielding* and *abrogating* suggest seemingly feminine postures for boys and men, mild derision could be said to offer them an acceptable—a subterranean and subversive—way to reclaim rather than repudiate the feminine within themselves while still saving face. As a result, humor becomes a reliable gauge of their deep gossip. This "good mockery of everyday life," Phillips asserts, "regulates our self-importance, and so relieves us of too much responsibility for the world" (40). It gives us a welcome break from ourselves.

As Capps (2002; 2005b; Dykstra, Cole, and Capps, 2007) points out in recent works on the religious and therapeutic functions of humor in boys' and men's lives, humor can remind especially those who hold to the high ideals of what he calls the religion of honor that they are *not* so different from everyone else. Humor connects them to, rather than isolates them from, their brothers. In ridiculing Rico's penis size and speculating on his frequent masturbation, Jimmy not only gives Rico permission to claim something of his own sexuality; he also tells Rico, in the coded but confessional language of humor, that he, Jimmy, is far more similar to Rico in this than different. And even Rico, at some unreflective level, would know this to be his friend's intended message.

Humor thus becomes a form of friendly fire among boys, a double-edged sword that sometimes maims and humiliates but that, among friends, as often cheers and fortifies. It allows boys to acknowledge and embrace on the sly a larger part of their personal experience. In Sherman Alexie's (2007) *The Absolutely True Diary of a Part-Time Indian*, mentioned at the beginning of the previous chapter, the banter between Arnold Spirit Jr. and his best friend Rowdy is filled with homosocial and homophobic referents utterly typical of and familiar to adolescent boys. But to the boys themselves, this give-and-take is unquestionably endearing and funny. Rowdy calls Arnold a "tree fag," and Arnold retorts by saying that he only sticks his "dick in girl trees." Later, Rowdy greets his friend by calling him a "dickwad," and Arnold comes back by telling him to kiss his ass. While humor always risks spilling over into abject humiliation, most boys know and demarcate the boundary between them. They respect as something sacred "a lot of jokes in the crotch area," clinging to their unique kind of humor as if to a spiritual lifeline.

If, as Phillips says, humiliation is the worst thing one can do to another, then a gentle, teasing humor among male friends—especially sexual humor at one's own or one's friend's expense—may be one of the best. It serves to inject an inert dose of humiliation as an inoculation against its more severe strains everywhere apparent in the inner and outer worlds of boys and young men. Mark Edmundson (2007), reflecting on Freud's last days of life, found in him the kind of curator of funny emotions who "had seen it all before, or imagined it. [Freud] freed people so that they could bear at first just to glance at their strangest wishes, and then to stare with a spirit of calm toleration *and even humor*" (104, emphasis added). Subverting the upward spiritualizing gaze of the church, humor brings boys and young men back down to earth, to *humus*, to the soil. It gives them back their bodies. It grounds them as incarnate souls.

For at least a fleeting moment, they can take comfort in acknowledging that they are boys who jerk off, even *a lot*.

## A HUMAN AND HUMANE JESUS
## AS SUBVERSIVE FRIEND

A third way for a curator of funny emotions to draw on the root *humus*, especially in relation to those adolescent boys and young men who identify as Christians—and in addition to doing everything possible to help them avoid humiliation and to recognizing and respecting their peculiar forms of humor as an inoculation against humiliation—would be to cultivate the notion of a *humble*, *human*, and *humane Jesus* as a prime candidate and guide for subversive friendship.

In the farewell discourse of the Gospel of John, Jesus is shown to assert that friendship, specifically friendship with him but also friendships modeled after his ("'Love one another . . . as I have loved you'" [13:34]), is the ultimate purpose of discipleship. One follows Jesus not to become his disciple but to become his, and by implication others', friend: "'I do not call you servants any longer, because the servant does not know what the master is doing; but I have called you friends, because I have made known to you everything that I have heard from my Father'" (15:15). Jesus' declaration runs counter to the church's usual tendency to prioritize Christian discipleship, however conceived, over every other human relationship. Instead, John paints Jesus as making friendship the main thing, making it, in a sense, everything. Especially here as a vulnerable, all-too-human man prematurely confronting death, Jesus wants and needs a friend; he wants and needs someone *to hang with*. Friendship is the point. It is the goal, the aim, the pinnacle of Christian love and discipleship. This, according to John's Gospel, is how Jesus hopes to be known, remembered, and loved—not as Lord or Master but as friend. There is no greater good, no grander spiritual purpose for which to strive, than the ordinary, costly, rewarding friendship that Jesus both seeks and affords. One becomes a Christian to aspire to friendship, to become a better friend.

Given, however, that boys and men, as Capps has noted, tend to resist thinking of themselves as religious or spiritual persons in any conventional sense, they are apt to experience difficulty if pressed to imagine Jesus as friend. But what if a curator of funny emotions were to reverse this thought experiment, asking them instead to think of an actual same-sex friend as Jesus? What if in the very act of teasing Rico about the magnifying glass and jerking off, Jimmy could be seen as actually having become in every sense Jesus to Rico? What if Rowdy's calling Arnold a "dickwad" were to be viewed in an equally redemptive light? In this reading of the farewell discourse, Jimmy and Rowdy would be interacting—not despite but because of their playful mockery—as Jesus would with Rico or Arnold, simply for being the kind of friends who can get away with deriding—and, in so doing, comforting—them in such an intimate, if indirect, way. It would follow from this perspective, in turn, that the prayer life of boys and young men could be seen as indistinguishable from, or simply another form of, their artfully coded and almost obligatory locker-room humor.

Asking them to think not of Jesus as their best friend but of their best friend as Jesus could prove liberating for Christian boys and men. Their spiritual life in this case would entail less a sober attempt to conjure and connect with a nebulous God in a far-flung heaven and more just hanging out and shooting the breeze with a close friend here on earth. Interactions with their friend would become for them in every sense encounters with Jesus or, at least, his nearest proxy. Crass, earthy, human, humane friendships would become the best, perhaps the only, laboratory in which to conceive and live out Christian love.

This view of Christian love is *not* meant to trivialize Christian discipleship as if it were some easy, well-trodden path to be taken for granted, for we have already seen how problem laden and elusive intimate same-sex friendships typically become as boys approach adulthood. Devoted male friendships are no less threatening, risky, and costly for reasons already noted—fear of physical arousal, emotional vulnerability, and claustrophobic self-depletion—than are more familiar conceptualizations of a life of faith. This reading of Jesus' farewell discourse *is*, however, to find in embodied, flesh-and-blood friendships the richest soil for nurturing Christian love. Friendship is important; it is urgent; it is complex; it is enough.

An article by *New York Times* columnist Bob Herbert (2008) may help to corroborate this point. He describes a course of friendship that is remarkable in part because it is in some ways so ordinary. It is a friendship between two young men in their mid-twenties, both survivors of devastating life circumstances. Herbert writes,

> Joshua Hubbell and Luis Rosa-Valentin were best friends at Meade Senior High School at Fort Meade, Maryland, just outside of Washington. Josh graduated in 2000 and Luis in 2001. Both of their dads were career soldiers. . . .
> A few years ago, Josh, who is now 26, learned that he had testicular cancer. "At that young age, you think you're invincible," he said. "The toll that it took mentally was just devastating." Luis, who had joined the Army . . . , was constantly on the phone with Josh, offering encouragement and moral support, helping his friend get through

the ordeal. "He still doesn't realize how much he helped me," Josh said. (A21)

Luis, an enthusiastic soldier who loved the Army, was sent to Iraq, where in April of 2008 he was blown up by an improvised explosive device. He lost an arm, both legs above the knee, and his hearing. He was flown to the Walter Reed Army Medical Center in Washington for treatment.

There, Josh started visiting his friend in the hospital each day. "Who was the tall young man, the quiet guy with the small wire-rimmed glasses," Herbert asks, "who was spending the entire day, every day, with the badly wounded soldier in room 5711?" The doctors, nurses, and attendants all wanted to know. "The people at the hospital were always asking, 'Who are you?'" [Josh] said. "And I'd say, 'I'm just his best friend.'"

Reflecting on the nature of the friendship of these two young men, Herbert concludes that "there is no use looking for words to explain the value of Josh's constant presence at Luis's bedside. The two men talk, play video games, watch movies, speculate about life and go through the good days and bad days together":

> "I suppose it's the meaning of love," Luis said. "I've got my best friend here helping me, and I need the help. I'm just extremely grateful to have a friend like Josh." Josh does not act as though he's doing anything extraordinary. "This is a fine way to spend my time," he said. "It's just nice to be able to hang out with him, after him being so close to being gone forever." (A21)

It seems unlikely that either of these young men would describe the motivation for their actions toward each other in particularly religious or spiritual terms. More likely, they would maintain that they do what they do because, as Josh says to the hospital staff, "I'm just his best friend," or because, as Luis says to the reporter, "I need the help." Neither of them would be so immodest as to claim to be Jesus or his stand-in in the life of the other. Perhaps neither calls himself a Christian.

All this notwithstanding, it seems plausible, justified, and even theologically necessary to recognize each friend as having functioned precisely as Jesus-made-flesh for the other in their respective travails. In their private, unemployed, unproductive, video-game-playing lives, one finds an unflinching devotion no less subversive of social conventions for men than was Jesus' own faithful subversion. Josh and Luis's unpretentious dedication *embodies* Jesus, reveals what Jesus *looks like*, all that Jesus *desires* and *intends*—humble, human, humane, one testicle and a few limbs shy of a cure but singular, omnipresent curators of each other's funny emotions nonetheless. Their friendship is the thing; it *is* their spiritual life, all-encompassing precisely in its particularity—one man's steady phone calls or the other's showing up every day at the hospital, both men's readiness to acknowledge the need for help and to receive it when offered.

About five months after Herbert's column on Josh and Luis appeared in the *New York Times*, I mentioned his account of their friendship in an address to a conference of pastoral counselors in Denver. Imagine my surprise when after my lecture I was approached by one of the counselors in the audience, who told me that only a month or so before he had spent a number of days with none other than Josh and Luis, beginning the very day Luis was discharged from the hospital. He explained that his work as a pastoral counselor almost exclusively entails leading intensive wilderness retreats for small groups of men, including on occasion wounded Iraq war veterans discharged from Walter Reed, at a vast working ranch in the Colorado Rockies. Through white-water rafting and other outdoor activities, including a skeet-shooting exercise in which Luis took particular delight, the retreats were crafted to strengthen men's capacity for intimacy with other men.

Randy, the pastoral counselor, told me that until my lecture he had not been aware of the *Times* article on their friendship or of Josh's daily visits to Luis in the hospital. He noted that the two men were relatively quiet during their days in the mountains and did not overtly speak of Christian faith. But what stood out about them, he said, was the ease of their presence with each other, particularly their comfort level as Josh tended his friend's physical needs. Theirs appeared to be, he told me, an honest, respectful, loving friendship. That week Josh helped Luis—only hours removed and thousands of miles away from the world of the hospital and absent his hearing, an arm, and both legs—to navigate treacherous waters.

The kind of embodied intimacy that set Josh and Luis apart in the eyes of a pastoral counselor who specializes in men's friendships does not come easily to young men in their twenties. It is not difficult to imagine that their wilderness wanderings, that week and since, must have involved learning to navigate not only the rushing white water of the Colorado mountains but the funny emotions that attend a young man's devotion to and need for another man, including somehow devotion to and need for his physical body. That Josh and Luis appear to have plunged into menacing waters of intimate same-sex friendship so much sooner and deeper than others of their peers—some of whom will never take that plunge—no doubt speaks to their respective experiences as vulnerable, all-too-human men prematurely confronting death. It speaks, as Josh puts it, to "him being so close to being gone forever." Facing circumstances not unlike those of Jesus in his final hours, other men evidently come to realize that, again in Josh's words, "it's just nice to be able to hang out with" a friend, "a fine way to spend [one's] time." In circumstances such as theirs, friendship is the thing.

Josh and Luis's bond, along with the bodily locus of Josh's cancer and the severity of Luis's injuries, almost certainly must have posed, and likely continue to pose, extreme threats to their versions of the masculine self. In addition, their exceptional friendship—given its particularity and exclusivity, its lack of productivity or of clear direction and purpose—confuses conventional categories of social commerce, of the primacy of the family, and of the priority of the community over the individual in Christian life and devotion. A friendship like theirs defies older boys' and men's ways of being with one another; it bends gender, raises eyebrows, and threatens self and social order. Despite, or perhaps because of, Josh's and Luis's humility and decency, theirs is a subversive friendship. This is why it goes almost without saying that they so fully appear to capture what Jesus must have had in mind in elevating friendship over servitude for those who would follow him. The very friendship that helped Josh and Luis to stave off death for the other, like friendship with Jesus, must have demanded of them other forms of dying and ushered in for them other kinds of death. Each has become the other's all-too-human, humane, perhaps even sufficient Jesus, a curator of funny emotions with a common ear for his friend's deep gossip.

# PART III

# Close Friendships

# 5

# Close Friendships

The chapters that precede this one have focused on the friendships that adolescent boys share with one another. In so doing, they support a major theme of William S. Pollack's *Real Boys' Voices* (2000), a sequel to his *Real Boys: Rescuing Our Sons from the Myths of Boyhood* (1998): adolescent boys' friendships with other boys are an extremely important aspect of their lives. We will be concerned in this chapter with the especially close or intimate friendship that one adolescent boy has with another adolescent boy.

Pollack's *Real Boys' Voices* is based on conversations that he had with dozens of teenage boys during a nationwide journey the summer of 1998. The book is organized into five parts titled "The Secret Emotional Lives of Boys," "The Cycle of Rage and Violence," "Boys Reaching Out and Connecting," "Dealing with Loss, Loneliness, and Shame," and "Boys in the World." In the part concerned with boys reaching out and connecting, there are chapters on "Love for Mother," "The Dad Connection," "Friendships and Romances with Girls," "Having Male Buddies," "Emotional Intensity: Connecting Through Sports," and "Coming Out as Gay and Supporting Those Who Do."

The chapter "Having Male Buddies" contains segments of conversations with five boys about their friendships with other boys. Pierre, a seventeen-year-old boy from a suburb in the Northwest, tells about his friendship with Eric, with whom he communicates very well. But he also mentions Kurt, "another close friend," with whom he went to elementary school. He says, "I can really, really feel open with him. We know each other's lives very intimately just because we have known each other since we were in kindergarten, and we can really talk freely and openly" (268). Graham, a seventeen-year old boy from a suburb in the West, says that if he is ever really upset he can talk to his "best friend Colin. It's so important to have a best friend" (270). This friendship also goes back to elementary school, and Graham can still remember the first day that he met Colin: "We were in fourth grade and it was right after winter break. He had been moving around a lot because his dad was in the navy. And we have been friends ever since" (271). He adds that the two of them "do literally everything together. Over the summer we will see each other six days out of the week. And we can each tell the other everything" (271). Clearly, being able to take the other into one's confidence is a fundamental, and the more one feels free to do so, the closer the relationship feels to him.

In a section of the chapter on the secret emotional lives of boys titled "Spirituality and Renewal," one of the segments is titled "The Closest Friend." William, a sixteen-year-old boy from the South, begins with this observation:

> Probably the hardest thing for a guy in high school these days is to keep a clear focus. It's a transition time, you're obviously growing up, looking ahead to college and decisions you have to make. Relationships with family, friends, girlfriends. I think that takes a big toll on some people. (102)

He goes on to relate how he has had "a lot of hard times" because, owing to his father's work, the family has moved four times:

> I was born in Oregon, then we moved to Vermont, to Charleston, back to Vermont, and down here to Florida just this past summer. Making these transitions is hard, and they have gotten harder as I've gotten older. In high school I think you are more connected with friends and school, you're more involved in everything. (103)

He explains that he "had a really close group of friends in Vermont," and that he liked the school he was going to. He keeps in touch with them by phone and e-mail.

But he also had a friend, Jake, with whom he was closer than the others, and this friend moved to Hong Kong while he was still up in Vermont. William was able to go visit him this past summer:

> We keep in touch a lot, and we tell each other pretty much everything. He is the person in my life that I've felt closest to. We would talk about anything. Spiritual struggles like sins, or when you're not seeing in your life what God wants, or it seems like he's just silent up there and does he even exist? Also just daily things that you share together, small things that strengthen a friendship. Girls, definitely. And also we pray for each other. That's a big part. We were very comfortable in being ourselves around each other, and I think that put us at a deep level. (103)

He goes on to say that he still has a friendship with Jake, and they keep in touch, but it's not the same as it was when they were together in Vermont. And there is no one in Florida that he is on the same level with. It's not that he's disappointed "because that was unique," but, he says, "It has definitely left a hole, and every day I feel it" (103).

William goes on to explain what, to him, makes a good relationship like the one he had with Jake:

> I think in order to be in a good relationship you have to be able to confidently be yourself. You don't have to try and change who you are to fit the other person's standards, and if it is a true friendship, the other person will accept that. Some people, though, have trouble acting like themselves. Maybe it's from trying to impress the other person, or trying to put yourself ahead of the person. I think everyone to a certain extent wants to elevate themselves, and I think that stifles a lot of friendships. (103–4)

With Jake, William was able to be himself. Jake accepted him for who he was. And if Jake had been able to listen in to the conversation, we can be certain that he would say he felt that William accepted *him* for who he was.

William indicates that he has not yet found a really close friend in Florida. One reason for this is that he runs up against the problem of conflicting values:

> I have different values—I don't drink or smoke or do drugs—and when I'm with friends who do these things, it's hard. There's a kind of a wall between the two of us when I say, "No, I'm not going to do that." We can't relate on that issue, which leaves me with mixed feelings. I'm glad that I don't give in to it, but also sad that I can't relate to that friend. In some ways it's almost impossible to get to that most intimate point of a friendship with them, because there's always going to be that difference unless one of you changes. It's hard, because I would want to be closer to that friend, but as far as personal integrity goes, I couldn't. (104)

One guesses that if he did make this change in order to have a close friendship, it would not feel close—at least, not like the closeness he experienced with Jake—because he would always feel that he had to change who he was and become someone different, and this would directly and negatively affect the closeness of their relationship.

As indicated, this segment from a conversation with William is not in the chapter on male buddies but in the chapter on spirituality and renewal. The reason for this is that William discusses his relationship to God, and, significantly, he uses much the same language here as he did when he told about his relationship to Jake. In fact, he makes the connection himself: "Having a relationship with God is like having the closest friend [because] I can always talk to God" (104). As in his conversations with Jake, he can talk with God about the bigger things in his life—like "college and the future"—but he can also talk with him about "just day-to-day things, like schoolwork that I'm struggling with. It's not like he's going to throw down a piece of paper with an A-plus on it, but he can provide encouragement for me to complete the everyday things as well as the big things" (104).

Of course, there's a difference too, for although God, like Jake, listens to his struggles and provides support, God also works his own will in William's life. This is also something that he treasures and relies on:

> I really do get encouragement knowing that he is caring for me and working in my life, that he actually does orchestrate my life through his will. . . . So I can almost give up to him the things that I'm strug-gling with. I mean, I can plan the future as much as I want, but he's going to make his will happen, so I have to be able to let myself fall back and just trust that he will work his way. That takes a lot of courage at times, and it's not easy to do, because as humans we want to hang on to every part of our life and be in control all the time. And you can't be. Moving to Florida this summer felt the most out of control for me, but I had God to fall back on and he brought me through it. . . . When you move, your whole life is just basically blown away, because if every aspect of your life changes, you have nothing to keep you who you are. You might lose all your values, because there's a barrage of new and different things that are open to you now. You have to have some kind of constant in your life, and for me, that's God. He keeps you together as your whole life changes. (105)

Although this difference between William's close friendship with Jake and with God is very significant, I am more interested here in the similarities, and in this regard, I would like to point to a similarity that William does not explicitly mention, but it is one that was probably very much on his mind as he went through the transition of moving from Vermont to Florida. This similarity arises from the fact that his relationship with Jake was not the same after Jake moved to Hong Kong. Although William was able to visit Jake the previous summer, their conversations now take place via e-mail and the tele-phone. They remain "close friends," but the very definition of what is meant by "close" has necessarily changed because they are not in immediate physical proximity with each other. As we saw in the case of the boys in the chapter on male buddies who talked about their close friendships, physical proximity was a critically important aspect of their sense of closeness. Graham, for example, sees Colin six days a week during the summer months. Knowing this friend for a long time is a very important factor in one's sense of closeness, but so is the fact that this friend is nearby and is therefore available to talk with whenever they feel the need to talk about something.

William says that his friendship with God is the "closest" friendship he now has, but it, too, is one where the friend is not physically present. When Jake was still in Vermont, they would talk about this very issue together, noting that they experienced times in their lives when it seemed like God was "just silent up there," and his silence caused them to wonder if he even existed. On the other hand, much like his continuing friendship with Jake despite the fact that Jake is in Hong Kong, he feels the very presence of God even though he cannot see God face to face. Acknowledging that "some people" say that talking to God is "not really two-way," he feels that he can "always talk to God" and know in his heart and mind that God is, in fact, listening. He explains:

> Prayer is how you can have a personal relationship with God, and that doesn't mean you have to stop and bow your head or go to church to pray. You can be thinking of God just as you walk through the halls: "Just help me be able to talk to this person nicely," or "I want to do your will in this decision. Let me know what that is." He doesn't always specifically say something, but a lot of times he'll make a decision clear. And just like a regular friendship, the more trials you go through together, the closer you become. Going through difficult moments in your life in a relationship with God brings you closer to God. (105)

Thus for William a key element in one's sense of closeness to God, despite the fact that one does not see God face to face, is that the two of you have gone through "difficult moments" together. An underlying assumption here is that God has William's best interests at heart and is not trying to make him into something that he is not.

This chapter on close friendships will focus on a *connection* that emerges from the association we have drawn between Pollack's chapters on male buddies and on spirituality and renewal, one that is illustrated by William's account of his close friendships with Jake and with God. In fact, in his introductory comments in the chapter on spirituality and renewal, Pollack uses the very language of connection that he employs in the part of the book that focuses on boys reaching out and connecting. He writes,

> One of the most inspirational experiences I had in my recent trek across the country, listening to and learning from America's boys and young men, is the large number of them—individuals from all walks of life—who feel a meaningful connection with a *spiritual* or religious force, an all-powerful presence outside themselves, a deeply caring being who is always there to listen to, love, and protect them. . . . For many boys, relating to a loving, forgiving, understanding spiritual

force can help sustain their sense of self, create a confidence and a strength that may be difficult to find elsewhere and may offer opportunities for renewal. (86)

This chapter will have an autobiographical focus, but I believe that readers will be able to derive insights from this account of my own life in much the same way that I have gained important insights from William's account of his life. Like William's story, mine will begin with a close friendship with a male buddy in my high school years, a friendship that like his, and unlike those of Pierre and Kurt and Graham and Colin, did not reach back into earlier childhood. In fact, one of the reasons that I found myself resonating with William's story is that I attended three high schools in four years due to my father's transfer to a new position in a city distant from where I had grown up. Also, like William's story, I feel that my story, despite the fact that it focuses on close friendships, would belong more in a chapter on spirituality and renewal than a chapter on having male buddies.

Unlike William's story, mine will be written, necessarily, from the perspective of an older man looking back on his adolescent years. Moreover, it will focus on a connection that I would consider spiritual or religious that Pollack does not identify (and there is no reason why he should have done so given the focus of his book on adolescent boys): namely, the connection between the older man and the adolescent boy he once was. Like William's relationship with God, this connection is an example of how there may be a close friendship despite their physical distance. Or to put it somewhat differently, there is a very real sense that the boy continues to live inside of the older man because they share common values and also have a sense that they have one another's interests at heart.

In light of the fact that our book focuses on boys' friendships with one another, it may seem a bit odd to include a chapter that focuses on a man's friendship with the boy who lives inside of him. One may justifiably ask, "What kind of friendship is *that*?" One might add with a critical tone, "Sounds pretty narcissistic to me." I hope, though, that this chapter will take a few steps toward answering the question and toward laying the second observation to rest. As for the question, I have already intimated that William's understanding of a close friendship will provide invaluable guidance toward answering it. As for the observation, I take my cue here from Pierre, who says that although he and Eric are close buddies, he thinks "it's also important that you don't get caught up too much with having one person and shut yourself off from everyone else. If you get everything from one person, you are not really going to know how to relate to others. And that's really not what you want" (Pollack 2000, 269). My point in this chapter, then, will be to suggest that *one* of the friends to whom we may turn is an earlier version of oneself. My one regret is that it took so many years to appreciate this simple truth. My discovery of this simple truth began with a failed attempt to find out what had happened to my best friend in my high school years.

## AN OVERDUE REUNION

In the fall of 2006 I received a mailing advising that I mark my calendar for a very important event: my high school class's fiftieth-year reunion party was approaching. The date had been set, and it was time to make reservations. A list of class members who were known to have died and another list of class-mates whose whereabouts were unknown were included in the mailing. We were asked to supply any information we might have about the latter so that they could be contacted and informed of the reunion party.

As I read through the list of those who had died, I had a sickening feeling not unlike the feeling that many have when they visit the memorial wall in Washington, D.C., for those who died in the Vietnam War. I was surprised that so many of the members of the class were no longer living. Then I read through the names of those who could not be located, and I had another reac-tion, as my best friend was on that list.[1]

I recalled that the last time I saw him was at our graduation ceremony. Neither of us made an effort to stay in touch after that. Despite the fact that his grades were excellent, he had decided not to go to college and would not be persuaded otherwise, while I was going to take courses at the local state college in the summer so that I could begin piling up credits in hopes of get-ting college over with as quickly as possible. I had no time for high school friends or, for that matter, for reflecting on my high school experience.

Now, fifty years later, I was not at all interested in attending the class reunion. I sent the class reunion committee a check to help defray the costs of the mailings and suggested to the committee treasurer that if the check didn't bounce, she would know that I was better off now that I had been in high school. A donation, a little joke—and I felt I was off the hook.

But the mailings kept coming—there was more information about the dress code at the country club where the dinner and dance were to be held, the fact that a tour of the high school had been arranged, and more requests for infor-mation about those whose whereabouts were unknown. My best friend had not been located. In fact, the list was essentially the same as the previous list had been. No one seemed to know the whereabouts of the missing, or if they knew, they had not taken the trouble to inform the reunion committee.

I thought of the fun (which we considered harmless) that my friend and I had had in the introductory journalism class that we signed up for in our junior year. We hadn't really known each other before this, but we began to walk home together and even attended a dance at the Presbyterian church near the high school (and learned on that occasion that we were very much out of our social depth). The seniors edited the school newspaper, but juniors were encouraged to submit copy. I wrote a rather straightforward editorial about not talking out loud in the library because it disturbs other students, and they accepted it.

Then, however, my friend and I came up with an idea. Each issue of the newspaper included a column devoted to the "Student of the Week." This was always a senior who was a member of the social elite, usually someone who was active in student government or on the football or basketball team. We noticed that quite a few dogs hung around the school and that they sometimes gained entry when someone opened a door. So we wrote a column on the "Canine of the Week," pretending that we had conducted an interview with the dog. We asked the dog the same questions that the newspaper reporter typically asked the student of the week. This meant asking dogs to identify their favorite teachers and classes, to tell us what college they planned to attend, to mention their favorite extracurricular activities (e.g., barking in the school choir), and relate their most embarrassing experience as high school students.

Typically, the answer to the last question by the student of the week would be along the lines of "My most embarrassing moment was the day when I slept in late, and in my rush to get to school on time, I put on a blue blouse with a green plaid skirt, only to discover this later. I was so embarrassed!" We asked the embarrassing question of Rex, a large mongrel who had a special knack for gaining entrance into the school. He replied that he has had many such moments, but the one that especially stood out in his mind was when he mistook a freshman for a fire hydrant.

For this seemingly harmless bit of humor we were called into the principal's office. He explained that students often take the school newspaper home and that parents read it. He also reminded us that the school had an excellent national reputation (it had received a commendation in a national magazine), and he did not want to place this in jeopardy. The interview concluded amicably, but we suspected that the journalism teacher had also been contacted by the principal because our canine-of-the-week column was no longer accepted by the seniors who ran the newspaper. Nor did the journalism teacher think it was amusing when we asked permission to leave the room—as other students often did—to conduct an interview with a seagull we had noticed from the window that was standing near the track. We wanted, we explained, to ask him if he was planning on trying out for the track team.

The reunion mailings—there were several more—began to weigh on me. I'd received college reunion mailings before, but these were summarily tossed into the waste basket without much thought. So, too, were reunion mailings from the schools where I had received advanced degrees. Why did I take the time to read the high school class reunion mailings? Why did it concern me that my best friend had not been located? After all, would I have contacted him if he had been found? I doubt it. So what was so special or unique about these class reunion mailings?

Several possible explanations occurred to me: One was that the high school years were themselves unique because these were years in which I felt that the biblical account of how the people of Israel wandered in the wilderness applied to me, as though my four high school years—at three different high schools—were roughly comparable to their forty years of wandering. Another was that my retirement as a professor was imminent, and the reunion mailings took me back in time to when my initial struggles to discover my vocation in life had begun. A third and related explanation was that, having announced my retirement a couple of years ahead of time, I was experiencing many of the same emotions that I had first experienced as a high school student: feeling marginal, isolated, directionless, and fearful of what the future held for me.

I found it rather incredible that a large number of my high school classmates would soon be gathering together to have dinner, to dance to the music of "our era," and tour the building where we had sat in classes, eaten lunch, gone to assemblies, and made fools of ourselves in the gymnasium, either trying to learn modern dance steps or to throw a ball into a ten-foot-high basket. Why would they want to relive those memories? Why would they risk meeting someone with whom they thought they were in love but who "dumped" them for someone else? Why would they chance seeing the guy who beat them out for a starting position on the varsity baseball team while they sat on the bench, game after game, trying their best to put the good of the team ahead of their own personal ambition and profound disappointment? Why would some of them risk the likelihood that no one would remember who they were or that they might find themselves without anyone to talk with?

I posed these questions to a friend who had recently attended his own fiftieth high school reunion party. Why did he go? Well, he had grown up in a working-class part of town, and he wanted his high school classmates to know that he had made good in his professional life. But, more importantly, the reunion committee had mentioned in one of their mailings that several of their teachers had agreed to attend the reunion dinner, and one of these teachers was a man who had inspired him to set his personal and vocational goals far beyond his working-class status. "Did you have a good time?" I asked. "Yes, I was able to impress a lot of people with what I did in life. On the other hand, I got into an argument with this one jerk because he wouldn't move to another table so that the teacher who meant so much to me could sit in a place of honor. He was a jerk then, and he's still a jerk."

It was not a very persuasive explanation for why someone would go to a high school reunion, but the very fact that it was not persuasive forced me to ask myself why this was so. This question then carried me back in time to the place where my wilderness wanderings had begun and to when I embarked on the perilous road to some far-off destination that held a great deal of promise but little by way of clarity or specificity. The fact that my best friend could not be located provided a useful clue to what I was feeling and, no doubt, resisting, for the reunion was not, after all, the issue. Rather, the real issue was that the high school boy who was somewhere deep inside of me was missing too. When I left high school with such finality and determination to get on with my life, I had left him behind—wandering about the empty halls, lost, as it were, in a kind of modern limbo not unlike the medieval version where, as Dante suggests, the lamentations of its occupants "are not the shrieks of pain, but hopeless sighs" (Le Goff 1984, 336; see also Capps and Carlin 2010).

But how should I go about finding him? Photos were somewhat helpful. Recollections stored in my mind were also useful. But in the end, I decided to consider what he wrote during his last two years in high school, specifically, a short story that was published in the national student magazine and a poem that was also written for a creative writing class.

In the following exploration, I will view these texts from the perspective of the older man who, years later, has found them valuable for making connections with the high school boy who continues to live inside of me. I will comment on these writings, treating them as respectfully as I would the writings of the students I have known throughout the years, but with no greater deference than *he* would have accorded them. In fact, my copy of the published short story (Capps 1957) has some handwritten changes of wording and phrasing, suggesting that he was not entirely happy with the published version.

## THE SHORT STORY: A BOY ON A MISSION

The story titled "Charlie" is set in western Nebraska. Some years earlier, our family had visited the Lutheran mission in Axtell where my cousin Christine had lived since birth, as my uncle and aunt had been advised that it was best to place Down syndrome children in an institution. I recall that my uncle was so distressed when he broke the news to my parents that their newborn daughter was "a Mongoloid" (the term that was used at the time for children with

Down syndrome) that I, four- or five years old at the time, asked my mother if she had died.[2]

While my parents visited with Christine and members of the staff, my brothers and I remained outside the building. We were entertained by a male resident who seemed to have some sort of mental abnormality. He asked us if we were from Funk, a nearby town, and when my father appeared, he patted my father's paunch and said, "I'll go get my ball too." His Funk query and his association of our father's paunch with a ball amused us so much that we often repeated the query—"You from Funk?"—when we happened to encounter one another, and we, too, would pat our father's stomach and say, "I'll go get my ball too."

This man became the main character in my story. I called him Charlie and represented him as a former farmer who was a resident in the mission but who left every morning to hang around in the town and then return to the mission later in the day. I suggested that he was frequently engaged in conversation with the boys in town, who enjoyed teasing him mildly, to which he would respond good-naturedly.

But on this particular morning he was in no mood for light banter. During the night, a young boy named Olav (a variant form of Olaf, a popular Scandinavian name) had found his way out of the mission building without anyone noticing and had disappeared. A rescue party had been formed, and when it failed to find him in town, it concentrated its efforts on the prairie beyond the town. Charlie told the boys that morning that he was worried about Olav: "'He ain't too strong, especially that game leg. Someone's got to do something.'" The boys didn't share his anguish: "'Why don't you? We gotta go catch rabbits. It's been nice talkin' with you.'" After they hurried off, Charlie continued talking to himself, mainly about needing a new milkweed to put into his mouth, then told himself that he would never be able to find Olav "jest talkin' here to myself," and he began walking.

Meanwhile, the mission chapel was filled with vigil keepers, many of whom expressed disbelief that Olav could have gone. Maybe he was only hiding, playing a trick as he had done so many times. Did someone search the barn where the old tomcat stays? Yes, "'but he wasn't there.'" Then the boys returned from chasing rabbits and found that Charlie was gone. "'Hey, where's crazy Charlie?'" No one seemed to know. They asked Jake, a kid who was hanging around, if he knew anything about what had happened to Charlie. He replied, "'Don't know. My dad says he took off mumbling that he thought Olav had something he had to find and that he thought he could help Olav find it.'"

The story shifts at this point to Charlie and his search for Olav. It reports that Charlie "walked on, through cornfields, over fences, and waded through streams and the Papio Creek, until he at last came to the bluff overlooking the mission. He turned, gazing back. They'll miss me at the mission, he thought. 'Maybe I oughta go back.'" Instead, he decided to keep going. "'No, Olav went exploring'," he told himself, "'and he'll find it. He knows, he's headed somewhere special.'"

At this point the narrator comments on the terrain, "One doesn't know how long a mile can be until he's walked a Nebraska mile, a sandy, dusty, choking mile," and says of Charlie,

> Cockleburs clung to his ankles and stung. The brush cut deeply into his leg, and he slowed down. He picked up a handful of sand and let it fall from his fingers. The prairie, rolling, rolling. A weary old man trudging, with a faraway look in his sun-squinted eyes—a look which seemed to pierce through things, deeply, compassionately. A crazy old man on a foolish trek, tired, almost to the point of giving in. He stumbled once and slowly raised himself. He looked over his shoulder and cried, "I won't be back!" It echoed through the cornfields until it whispered through the mission gate, "I won't be back." Charlie's gone. He went to find the boy, Olav. He won't be back. He won't be back. And on he trudged. And the sand sifted slowly through his clutching hand, the sun settled silently on the treeless bluff, and a weary man stumbled and fell to the ground with that faraway look in his tear-glistened eyes. "Olav, I've found you! Don't wait for me. I'm catching up, Olav, my boy, I've found you." The sun sank slowly on the quiet bluff, and the sand no longer sifted through his clutching hand.

With this, the story ends.

I am not concerned here with evaluating the story as a piece of creative writing. Instead, my interest lies in what the story tells me about the high school boy who wrote it. With this in mind, I would especially take note of the narrator's emphasis on the fact that Olav did not wander off the mission grounds for no good reason. Rather, there was a purpose to his decision to leave the mission. In effect, he was *on* a mission. He was embarking on a quest, headed, as Charlie perceived, "somewhere special." Also, because the mission was all that he had ever known, this "somewhere special" was not the home where he had lived prior to becoming a resident at the mission. This "somewhere special" serves as an image of hope (see Lynch 1965; Capps 2001, 64–71). This image is intentionally undefined. The narrator does not say, for example, that the boy's quest was for heaven or that he was drawn by the magnetism of God. As the reader, I am rather pleased that the narrator left the object of the boy's quest indistinct, because an effort to identify it more precisely would have made the story overtly religious. There were already enough religious associations in the story with its references to the mission and, more specifically, the mission chapel where the vigil keepers had gathered.

A second observation concerns the relationship of the old man and the young boy. The story reverses the usual expectation that the older man is the one who leads and the young boy is the one who follows. Not here. The old man is drawn by the power of the boy, who is in quest of "something special." But, as the story comes to a close, the old man does not say that he, too, wants what the boy is searching for. Instead, he declares, "'Olav, I've found you! Don't wait for me. I'm catching up. Olav, my boy, I've found you.'" His search is for the boy himself. But he doesn't want the boy to wait for him. Instead, he wants Olav to keep going, and he will do the catching up. As he lies on the ground, he declares that he has, in fact, found the boy.

As I view the story from my vantage point as an older man, I have a deep sense of being Charlie, with the story's author being Olav. An older man is tempted to view his younger self as struggling to discover what the older man, through time and effort, has managed to find for himself. But the Charlie of the story is far wiser than this. He understands that it is the boy who is out ahead, searching for what he knows. Charlie is the one who is trying to catch up. On the other hand, the significant thing is that they are both traveling the same path in the same direction with the same destination out in front of them.

If the author of the story identifies with Olav, we can't avoid thinking that he finds his current situation—a boy who spends much of his life in a school—rather confining. In fact, as the story was written in my junior year, it may well be significant that in my senior year I enrolled in a special program called "distributive education," which was designed for boys who were not planning to attend college but were, instead, intending to enter the work world after graduation. Students enrolled in this program would attend classes half a day and work part-time jobs in the afternoon. Mine was a custodial job in a nearby hospital.

This identification with Olav may also shed light on my failure to remain in touch with my closest friend despite the fact that the two of us continued to live in the same city. There was a sense in which I, like Olav, was on a spiritual quest whose destination would have been obscure to everyone else but that entailed leaving everything that I had known and valued in my life behind, including this special friendship. Like the old man in the story, I do not view this as a mere rejection of the past and the relationships that had been important to me, but rather as an expression of what Gordon W. Allport (1950) calls "the solitary way," a person's "audacious bid" to bind oneself "to creation and to the Creator," an "ultimate attempt to enlarge and to complete his own personality by finding the supreme context in which he rightly belongs" (141–42). As noted, Olav is on a mission—a solitary quest—and it does not occur to him that he might encourage one of his friends in the mission to join him. And this brings me to the poem.

## THE POEM

This poem was one of several poems I wrote for a creative writing class in my senior year. They were all sonnets, a poetic form that I had become quite fond of because of its relative brevity (fourteen lines) but also because there was the expectation of a turning point between the eighth and ninth line. It suggested that what had been written to this point would be viewed from a different perspective in the subsequent lines. Here is the poem:

> *Roads to Emmaus*
> There are means of bringing back to life besides
> squeezing reluctant breath from agèd hearts,
> other ways than dreams, rehearsing parts
> of yesterday less vigor, than tides
> circling earth at intervals—perhaps they
> but reverse intention. No, we desire
> birth not wholly new lest critics say
> we despise order. Yet the times require
> more than repetition: the sudden burst
> of tears when it occurs to us the Word
> we sought went past when we conversed
> tonight. The terror of it all
> that resurrection waited our recall,
> the wonder not the life but that we heard.

Here, the poet identifies with one of the travelers on the road to Emmaus who was engaging in conversation with his companion about what had recently taken place in Jerusalem. He reflects on the fact that the Stranger who joined them reminded them of what the prophets had said and that the resurrection depended on their recall. He contrasts the terror of this thought—what if there had been no stranger-assisted recall?—with the wonder of the fact that they were able to hear the Word as the Stranger spoke with them. As Luke 24:32 puts it, "They said to each other, 'Were not our hearts burning within us while he was talking to us on the road, while he was opening the scriptures to us?' "[3]

As I read this poem after receiving the series of mailings about my high school reunion, I initially wondered why I titled it "Roads to Emmaus." Why the plural form? As I was quite certain that I would have been acquainted with Robert Frost's poem, "The Road Not Taken" (Frost 1969, 105), I wondered if this poem was on my mind when I wrote my own poem. But if so, there is an important difference between the two poems. In Frost's poem the roads lead to very different destinations, but in this poem there are alternative ways to get to the same destination. And perhaps this adds to the poem's sense of uncertainty and tenuousness: "What if the Stranger had taken a different road to Emmaus?"

In any event, the poet himself seems especially interested in the fact that the illumination or clarity occurs to the two travelers after the Stranger is gone, when they said to one another, "Were not our hearts burning within us when he was talking to us on the road, while he was opening the scriptures to us?" He suggests, however, that there may well have been another emotional response besides that of burning hearts: "The sudden burst / of tears when it occurs to us the Word / we sought went past when we conversed / tonight." Then he adds that there is something terrifying about the very fact "that resurrection waited our recall, / the wonder not the life but that we heard." In other words, truth requires that someone speak, but it also requires that those who are spoken to be able to see who it is that is talking to them and to hear what he has to say to them.

My comments on the short story would suggest that the poet here does not have anyone specific in mind as his companion on the road to Emmaus. It is conceivable that he was thinking as he wrote the poem about his closest friend and that they were on this journey together. I tend, however, to doubt that, especially because what Pollack calls "a spiritual or religious force" was rarely a topic of discussion between them. But this very absence of a clearly identified companion frees me, as the older man who is reading this poem, to suggest that I might take the role of the companion and join this adolescent boy on his pilgrimage to Emmaus.

As I do so, I find myself listening to him as he relates the various ways in which life or what has gone before might be recovered or regained—such as by attempting to reinvigorate the flagging hearts of those who are old and tired, or by means of dreams that rehearse parts of yesterday without their original vigor, or by the ebb and flow of tides. And I find myself agreeing with him that these methods merely repeat the past while we desire some form or expression of rebirth—not a rebirth that has no connection or association with the past or that flies in the face of order, but something new and unprecedented. He tells me that this is what we experienced earlier tonight when the Stranger revealed himself to us—or, more accurately, what we experienced *after* the Stranger had disappeared from our midst, for only then did we hear and understand what had been disclosed to us.

In one sense, there is nothing that the young poet is telling me that I did not know already for, after all, he was simply saying in his own words what the author of the Gospel of Luke had already told us. But there is something in the way he says it—in words and phrases that are, in a sense, expressive of the birthing event to which they refer. To my now older ears, the key words are *tears*, *terror*, and *wonder*—words that, together, convey the sense of an overwhelming mixture of emotions befitting the depth and enormity of the experience that they could not have anticipated in a thousand years, much less made any preparation for.

As I listen to this boy, I feel that I can relate to him—I feel a closeness that I do not expect others to feel because, after all, they do not know him as I know him. This closeness is partly due to the fact that I know that he worked this short story and this poem over and over again in his mind, struggling to say what he felt in his heart. We *could* say that he was trying to put his faith into words, but if we did, he would probably have felt a fair degree of irritation because this way of putting it sounds simplistic and trite. Moreover, his very choice of the sonnet form reflects his desire to achieve a congruence of structure and content—for he is concerned to present an understanding of the new life in an orderly way, but not at the expense of the very sense of innovation and vigor that this new life exhibits and promotes.

I believe I can also say that if I were his traveling companion on this road to Emmaus, I would not have expected that he would have had a great deal to say. In fact, for much of the initial stages of the journey, he would have been lost in thought. So I may have felt a certain relief that the Stranger came along and enlivened our walk by engaging us both in spirited conversation. But I also believe that I would have felt that the young boy possessed a predominant sense of calm, not unlike the natural world on either side of the road, and in spite of the excitement and turmoil of recent events.

## THE YOUNG MENTOR

In the epilogue of *Real Boys' Voices*, Pollack (2000) discusses the need of adolescent boys for safe places where they can go to be their real selves and for mentors on whom they can rely for guidance, love, and support (383–84). By "mentor" he does not mean only men, for a mentor can be a person of either gender. Also, although this mentor is most typically an adult, a mentor may also be another adolescent boy or girl either older or the same age as himself. What is a mentor? Pollack explains:

> This must be a person who listens to him without judgment when he is afraid or in pain; cheers him on as he goes about finding his place in the world; gives him a hug when he feels disappointed in a grade or a game, heartbroken over a troubled friendship, worried or sad about a loss in his life, or disconnected from friends or family. (384)

Pollack does not envision that this mentor would be younger than the boy, but it occurs to me that in light of the fact that a boy may have two, three, or several mentors, perhaps one of them might be a younger boy on whom the older, adolescent boy can rely for guidance, love, and support. Furthermore, it is not entirely far-fetched to suggest that this younger boy might be a younger version of this older boy.

A few years before the preceding short story and poem were written, I wrote the following poem about a season that others have tended to disparage:

*Winter*
Winter is a joyful season
It is joyful—there's a reason.
Ice and snow and outdoor fun
Cozy nights when play is done.

Each day more fun than all the rest.
I know—for this day is the best.
But Mother now has called us in.
I wish tomorrow would begin.

It would be easy for us to say that this younger boy—a nine- or ten-year-old—is in for a rude awakening, that there will come a day when the anticipated tomorrow is worse than today, which is already bad enough. But why should we assume that he is utterly naive when, more likely, he is a boy with an irrepressible will to believe (James 1992)? And if this is so, there is a sense in which he was the older adolescent boy's mentor.

And if the younger boy can be a mentor to the older boy, is it not also the case that the older adolescent boy can be a mentor to the older man? Of course, the adolescent boy is much younger. On the other hand, he was there earlier. Moreover, the very needs and struggles that Pollack identifies—being afraid or in pain, struggling to find his place in the world, disappointment in the outcome of a activity or task in which he was personally engaged, heartbroken over a troubled friendship, worried or sad about a loss in his life, disconnected from friends or family—are not unique to adolescence. The older man experiences these too, and he has a similar need for someone to listen, to cheer him on, and to give him a hug (whether literally or metaphorically).

So, in effect, this account of the older man having come to befriend the adolescent boy who lives inside of him comes down to this: The adolescent boy has proven to be a trustworthy guide on the older man's life journey. Crazy Charlie understood this. He knew that Olav knew the way, and he chose to follow him. In this regard, Charlie was profoundly wise.

## CONCLUDING REFLECTIONS

In the introduction, we alluded to Ralph Waldo Emerson's (1983) essay titled "Friendship." I believe that what the boys in Pollack's (2000) *Real Boys' Voices* had to say about their close friendships supports what Emerson says about friendship, especially his view that friendship has two basic elements: *truth* and *tenderness*.

Over and over again, these boys emphasize that their close friends are persons they could tell everything and not feel any need or desire to hold anything back. As Graham says of his conversations with Colin: "I have no shame with Colin; I can literally tell him anything and he can tell me as well" (Pollack 2000, 271). They also emphasize that it is virtually impossible to have really close friendships with boys who do not accept them as they truly are, or in which they feel that they are required to adapt to a value system with which they are uncomfortable. Thus, truth is essential, and an important aspect of this truth is that one can be oneself. In fact, a close friendship is a means toward coming to know who one is, for, as Emerson also points out, "We must be our own before we can be another's" (351).

There is also a deep sense of tenderness in the ways in which these boys talk about their close friends. No doubt, this tenderness would come through even stronger in the tone of their voices than it does in what they say. Also, several of the boys whose conversations are presented in the chapter on having male buddies mention that boys do not find it easy to share their feelings with others. But this very fact makes their accounts of occasions when a boy came to them and cried over a broken relationship with a girl, or about the fact that a friend gets really down and seems depressed stand out even more. No doubt, if their close friends had been the ones with whom Pollack talked, they would have reported times when *they* were the ones who cried or seemed depressed. What comes through in these conversations is that the boys genuinely care about their close friends, and they know in their hearts that their close friends care about them. And especially in these two ways—truth and tenderness—their friendships support Emerson's view that "the essence of friendship is entireness, a total magnanimity and trust" (354).

Pollack's conversation with William, a segment of which is recorded in his chapter on spirituality and renewal, also supports Emerson's view that friendship "demands a religious treatment" because it is truly a gift from God and therefore one of the beautiful ways in which God shows himself. William understands this when he suggests that Jake is his close friend and God is his closest friend. This means, however, that a close friendship requires reverence and should not be treated casually. In fact, too often, "Our friendships hurry to short and poor conclusions, because we have made them a texture of wine and reams, instead of the tough fiber of the human heart" (Emerson 1983, 345). Boys like Graham and William know that a close friendship is not to be exploited for utilitarian purposes. A close friend is not to be used. On the other hand, a close friend offers support, especially in times of disappointment, uncertainty, and despair.

If all of this is true, we might wonder why some—perhaps many—of these friendships do not continue after the boys leave high school. William, I believe, provides one important explanation for this: he and Jake were no longer living in Vermont. I think the fact that both of them moved away from Vermont was critically important in this regard, for if William had continued to live in Vermont he could provide Jake reports of what was happening there. By their moving to Florida and Hong Kong, both lost contact with the place where their friendship had grown. Emerson likens a friendship to a plant that is deeply rooted in the soil and that takes its own time to grow and to flower. When adolescent boys form close friendships, they do so knowing that they will sooner or later leave home and more than likely embark on a solitary journey toward different destinations. Will their friendship survive this experience of uprooting? Perhaps, but if it does not, a boy should not blame himself. As several of the boys in Pollack's study point out, boys tend to be too hard on themselves.

In the introduction, we cited the friendship of David and Jonathan as an example of a friendship that exemplified the three forms of friendship we have discussed in this book: the faithful friendship, the subversive friendship, and the close friendship. In light of what I have just said about the possibility—even the likelihood—that a close friendship formed in the adolescent years may not survive its uprooting, I would like to conclude this chapter with a poem by John Henry Newman (Newman 1888, 115–16).

*David and Jonathan*
"Thy love to me was wonderful, passing the love of women."
O Heart of Fire! Misjudged by willful man,
Thou flower of Jesse's race!
What woe was thine, when thou and Jonathan
Last greeted face to face!
He doomed to die, thou on us to impress
The portent of a blood-stain'd holiness.

Yet it was well:—for so, 'mid cares of rule
And crime's encircling tide,
A spell was o'er thee, zealous one, to cool
Earth-joy and kingly pride;
With battle-scene and pageant, prompt to blend
The pale calm spectre of a blameless friend.

Ah! Had he lived, before thy throne to stand
Thy spirit keen and high
Sure it had snapp'd in twain love's slender band
So dear in memory;
Paul of his companion reft, the warning gives,—
He lives to us who dies, he is but lost who lives.

Here, Newman suggests that with his ascension to the throne David assumed the demeanor and attitude of a king, making it difficult if not impossible for Jonathan to be in David's company knowing that their positions would have been reversed were it not for his graceful spirit. To support his point, Newman alludes to the sharp disagreement between Paul and Barnabas over whether or not to take John Mark with them on their next missionary journey (Acts 15:36–41), a dispute that led to their separation.

This allusion to Paul in a poem about David and Jonathan suggests that there are various ways in which a close friendship can end in separation. But these two examples seem to illustrate the two most common reasons besides the loss of close physical proximity for the separation between two close friends in the adolescent years: Either one of them changes due to positive events in his life that give him a higher status or position, thereby making the situation uncomfortable for the one who is less successful; or their friendship is disrupted when a third person—typically another boy or a girlfriend—becomes important in the life of one of them. In effect, Newman's poem tells us that a close friendship will not survive if either truth is compromised or tenderness is stifled. But even in the case of friendships that do not survive the adolescent years, let us not forget that for most of these boys friendship is "the solidest thing" they know (Emerson 1983, 346).

# Notes

## Introduction

1. An illustration from our first book (Dykstra, Cole, and Capps 2007) is Robert Dykstra's account of "a contaminating friendship" (37–39).
2. Joseph Scriven, who was born in Ireland in 1819 and emigrated to Canada in 1844, wrote a poem titled "Pray Without Ceasing" in 1855 as a comfort to his mother when he learned of her serious illness. It was published in a collection of his poems in 1869. That same year, Charles C. Converse, an American lawyer and composer, on discovering the poem, wrote the music for it, and the first line became the title of the hymn. http://en.wikipedia.org/wiki/Joseph_M._Scriven and http://www.suite101.com/content/what-a-friend-we-have-in-jesus-a57293. Retrieved September 4, 2010.

## Chapter 1: Faithful Friendships

1. Recognizing this fact does not preclude also recognizing that baseball provided Ken with friendships that offered him support and pleasure.

## Chapter 2: Friendship as Boyhood Spirituality

1. Much of the following discussion of identity and identity crisis appears in Cole (2009, 531–49).
2. These may also be sought and reexperienced in religion and its rituals, in ways that I have detailed in Cole (2009), previously cited.

## Chapter 4: Friendly Fire

1. See, for example, Davidson (2001, 40–46); Dykstra (2005); Eilberg-Schwartz (1991, 141–76; 1994, esp. 59–133); Friedman (2001, 1–54); Gollaher (2000, 1–52); Haldeman (1996); and Steinberg (1983/1996).

## Chapter 5: Close Friendships

1. This is not the friend I told about in our earlier book, *Losers, Loners, and Rebels* (Dykstra, Cole, and Capps 2007, 167–69). As my family had moved to another

city when I was a high school freshman, I needed to make new friends. On the other hand, there is a certain similarity in the two relationships because the second, as with the first, was a reflection of what I called the "soft rebel" (162–72).

2. In a scrapbook compiled in 1948 (when I was nine years old) there is a list that I had typed of thirty-seven dates to remember, most relating to the birth dates of U.S. presidents. But two entries stand out—one indicates that National Child Health Day is May 1; the other notes that the first orphanage in the United States opened on August 7, 1727. It appears that I was very concerned about my cousin's health and her institutionalization.

3. It is very likely that as the Stranger opened the Scriptures to them, he also opened them to truths about themselves that they had forgotten or never really known. As Julia Kristeva points out in *Strangers to Ourselves* (1991), the stranger who comes to us as "the other" may remind us of what we have forgotten or repressed in ourselves (183–93).

# References

Abelove, Henry. 2003. *Deep Gossip*. Minneapolis, MN: University of Minnesota Press.

Alexie, Sherman. 2007. *The Absolutely True Diary of a Part-Time Indian*. New York: Little, Brown & Co.

Allport, Gordon W. 1950. *The Individual and His Religion*. New York: Macmillan.

Apatow, Judd. 2007. *Superbad* [Film]. Culver City, CA: Columbia Pictures.

———. 2009. *Funny People* [Film]. Los Angeles: Universal Studios.

Augustine, St. 1960. *The Confessions of Saint Augustine*. Translated by John K. Ryan. Garden City, NY: Doubleday Image Books.

Baldwin, James. 1985/2001. "Here Be Dragons." In *Traps: African American Men on Gender and Sexuality*, ed. R. P. Byrd and B. Guy-Sheftall, 207–18. Bloomington, IN: Indiana University Press.

Baker, Russell, ed. 1986. *The Norton Book of Light Verse*. New York: W. W. Norton.

Blow, Charles M. 2009. "Two Little Boys." *New York Times*, April 24, 2009, http:// blow.blogs.nytimes.com/2009/04/24/two-little-boys/. Retrieved March 7, 2012.

———. 2010. "Don't Tickle Me, Bro!" *New York Times*, March 13, 2010, http://www .nytimes.com/2010/03/13/opinion/13blow.html. Retrieved September 4, 2010.

Boyarin, Daniel. 1995. *Carnal Israel: Reading Sex in Talmudic Culture*. Berkeley, CA: University of California Press.

Brown, Peter. 1988/2008. *The Body and Society: Men, Women, and Sexual Renunciation in Early Christianity*. New York: Columbia University Press.

Buczynski, Alan. 1992. "Iron Bonding." *New York Times Magazine* (July 19). MM12.

Capps, Donald. 1957. "Charlie." *Literary Cavalcade* 9:14–15.

———. 1970. "John Henry Newman: A Study of Religious Leadership." PhD diss., University of Chicago.

———. 1972. "A Biographical Footnote to Newman's 'Lead, kindly light.'" *Church History* 41: 1-7.

———. 1983. "Parabolic Events in Augustine's Autobiography." *Theology Today* 40: 260-72.

———. 1990a. "Augustine's *Confessions*: The Scourge of Shame and the Silencing of Adeodatus." In *The Hunger of the Heart: Reflections on the* Confessions of

Augustine, ed. Donald Capps and James E. Dittes, 69-92. West Lafayette, IN: Society for the Scientific Study of Religion.

———. 1990b. "Life Cycle Theory and Pastoral Care." In *Dictionary of Pastoral Care and Counseling*, ed. Rodney J. Hunter, 648-51. Nashville, TN: Abingdon Press.

———. 1990c. *Reframing: A New Method in Pastoral Care*. Minneapolis, MN: Fortress Press.

———. 1992. "Religion and Child Abuse: Perfect Together." *Journal for the Scientific Study of Religion* 31: 1-14.

———. 1993. *The Depleted Self: Sin in a Narcissistic Age*. Minneapolis, MN: Fortress Press.

———. 1995. *The Child's Song: The Religious Abuse of Children*. Louisville, KY: Westminster John Knox Press.

———. 1997. *Men, Religion, and Melancholia*. New Haven, CT: Yale University Press.

———. 1998. *Living Stories: Pastoral Counseling in Congregational Context*. Minneapolis, MN: Fortress Press.

———. 2000. *Deadly Sins and Saving Virtues*. Eugene, OR: Wipf & Stock Publishers.

———. 2001a. *Agents of Hope: A Pastoral Psychology*. Eugene, OR: Wipf & Stock Publishers.

———. 2001b. *Giving Counsel: A Minister's Guidebook*. St. Louis, MO: Chalice Press.

———. 2002. *Men and Their Religion: Honor, Hope, and Humor*. Harrisburg, PA: Trinity Press International.

———. 2003. *Biblical Approaches to Pastoral Counseling*. Eugene, OR: Wipf & Stock Publishers. (Orig. pub. 1981.)

———. 2005a. "Nervous Laughter: Lament, Death Anxiety, and Humor." In *Lament: Reclaiming Practices in Pulpit, Pew, and Public Square*, ed. Sally A. Brown and Patrick D. Miller, 70-79. Louisville, KY: Westminster John Knox Press.

———. 2005b. *A Time to Laugh: The Religion of Humor*. New York: Continuum.

———. 2006a. "Desire Faileth Not." *The Journal of Pastoral Care & Counseling* 60:161-64.

———. 2008a. "Aging Horses and Wounded Healers." *The Journal of Pastoral Care & Counseling* 62: 293-96.

———. 2008b. *Laughter Ever After . . . Ministry of Good Humor*. St. Louis, MO: Chalice Press.

———. 2008c. *The Decades of Life: A Guide to Human Development*. Louisville, KY: Westminster John Knox Press.

Capps, Donald, and Nathan Carlin (2010). *Living in Limbo: Life in the Midst of Uncertainty*. Eugene, OR: Wipf & Stock Publishers.

Coble, Richard. 2010. "Loser as Subversive Friend: A Case Study in Youth Ministry." Unpublished manuscript, Princeton Theological Seminary, Princeton, NJ.

Cole, Allan Hugh Jr. 2008. *Be Not Anxious: Pastoral Care of Disquieted Souls*. Grand Rapids: Wm. B. Eerdmans Publishing Co.

———. 2009. "Male Melancholia, Identity-loss, and Religion." *Pastoral Psychology* 58: 531–49.

Cooper, Arnold M. 2005. "What Men Fear: The Façade of Castration Anxiety." In *The Quiet Revolution in American Psychoanalysis: Selected Papers of Arnold M. Cooper*, ed. Elizabeth L. Auchincloss, 150–62. New York: Brunner-Routledge.

Cuarón, Alfonso. 2001. *Y Tu Mamá También* [Film]. Mexico City: Twentieth-Century Fox.

Culbertson, Philip L. 1992. *New Adam: The Future of Male Spirituality*. Minneapolis: Fortress Press.

———. 1994. *Counseling Men*. Minneapolis: Fortress Press.

———. 1996. "Men and Christian Friendship." In *Men's Bodies, Men's Gods: Male Identities in a (Post-) Christian Culture*, ed. Björn Krondorfer, 149–80. New York and London: New York University Press.

Davidson, Arnold I. 2001. *The Emergence of Sexuality: Historical Epistemology and the Formation of Concepts*. Cambridge, MA: Harvard University Press.

Diamond, Lisa M. 2008. *Sexual Fluidity: Understanding Women's Love and Desire*. Cambridge, MA: Harvard University Press.

Dowd, Maureen. 2008. "An Ideal Husband." *New York Times*, July 6, 2008, A10, http://www.nytimes.com/2008/07/06/opinion/06dowd.html.

Dykstra, Robert C. 2005. "Rending the Curtain: Lament as an Act of Vulnerable Aggression." In *Lament: Reclaiming Practices in Pulpit, Pew, and Public Square*, ed. Sally A. Brown and Patrick D. Miller, 59–69. Louisville, KY: Westminster John Knox Press.

Dykstra, Robert C., Allan Hugh Cole Jr., and Donald Capps. 2007. *Losers, Loners, and Rebels: The Spiritual Struggles of Boys*. Louisville, KY: Westminster John Knox Press.

Edmundson, Mark. 2007. *The Death of Sigmund Freud: The Legacy of His Last Days*. New York: Bloomsbury USA.

Eilberg-Schwartz, Howard. 1991. *The Savage in Judaism: An Anthropology of Israelite Religion and Ancient Judaism*. Bloomington: Indiana University Press.

———. 1994. *God's Phallus and Other Problems for Men and Monotheism*. Boston: Beacon Press.

Emerson, Ralph Waldo. 1983. *Emerson: Essays and Lectures*, ed. Joel Porte, 62. New York: The Library of America.

Erikson, Erik H. 1958. *Young Man Luther: A Study in Psychoanalysis and History*. New York: W. W. Norton & Co.

———. 1964. *Insight and Responsibility*, 109-57. New York: W. W. Norton & Co.

———. 1968/1994. *Identity, Youth and Crisis*. New York: W. W. Norton & Co.

———. 1969. *Gandhi's Truth: On the Origins of Militant Nonviolence*. New York: W. W. Norton & Co.

———. 1977. *Toys and Reasons: Stages in the Ritualization of Experience*. New York: W. W. Norton & Co.

———. 1980/1994. *Identity and the Life Cycle*. New York: W. W. Norton & Co. (Orig. pub. 1959.)

———. 1981. "The Galilean Sayings and the Sense of 'I'". *The Yale Review* 70: 321-62.

———. 1987a. "Psychosocial Identity." In Erik H. Erikson, *A Way of Looking at Things*, ed. Stephen Schlein, 675-84. New York: W. W. Norton & Co.

———. 1987b. "The Human Life Cycle." In Erik H. Erikson, *A Way of Looking at Things*, ed. Stephen Schlein, 595-617. New York: W. W. Norton & Co.

Freud, Sigmund. 1917/1963. "Mourning and Melancholia." In Sigmund Freud, *General Psychological Theory: Papers on Metapsychology*, ed. Philip Rieff. Translated by Joan Riviere, 164–79. New York: Collier Books.

———. 1926/1959. *Inhibitions, Symptoms, and Anxieties*. In *The Standard Edition of the Complete Psychological Works of Sigmund Freud*, ed. James Strachey, vol. 20, 77–175. Translated by James Strachey. London: Hogarth Press.

———. 1930/1961. *Civilization and Its Discontents*. In *The Standard Edition of the Complete Psychological Works of Sigmund Freud*, ed. James Strachey, vol. 21, 59–148. Translated by James Strachey. London: Hogarth Press.

———. 1937/1964. "Analysis Terminable and Interminable." In *The Standard Edition of the Complete Psychological Works of Sigmund Freud*, ed. James Strachey, vol. 23, 209–54. Translated by James Strachey. London: Hogarth Press.

Friedman, David M. 2001. *A Mind of Its Own: A Cultural History of the Penis*. New York: Penguin Books.

Fromm, Erich. 1994. *The Art of Listening*. New York: Continuum.

Frost, Robert. 1969. *The Poetry of Robert Frost: The Collected Poems, Complete and Unabridged*, ed. Edward Connery Latham. New York: Holt, Rinehart and Winston.

Garber, Marjorie. 2000. *Bisexuality and the Eroticism of Everyday Life*. New York: Routledge.

Gilligan, Carol. 1982. *In a Different Voice: Psychological Theory and Women's Development*. Cambridge, MA: Harvard University Press.

Ginsberg, Allen. 1996. "City Midnight Junk Strains." In *Selected Poems, 1947–1995*. New York: HarperCollins.

Gollaher, David L. 2000. *Circumcision: A History of the World's Most Controversial Surgery*. New York: Basic Books.

Grimes, William. 2010. "Alice Miller, Psychoanalyst, Dies at 87; Laid Human Problems to Parental Acts." *New York Times*, April 27, 2010, http://nytimes.com/2010/04/27us27miller.html.

Haldeman, Scott. 1996. "Bringing Good News to the Body: Masturbation and Male Identity." In *Men's Bodies, Men's Gods: Male Identities in a (Post-) Christian Culture*, ed. Björn Krondorfer, 111–24. New York and London: New York University Press.

Herbert, Bob. 2008. "The Man in the Room." *New York Times*, June 17, A21.

Hijuelos, Oscar. 2008. *Dark Dude*. New York: Atheneum Books.

James, William. 1992a. "The Importance of Individuals." In *William James: Writings 1878–1899*, ed. Gerald Myers, 647–52. New York: Library of America. (Orig. pub. 1896.)

———. 1992b. "The Will to Believe." In *William James: Writings 1878–1899*, ed. Gerald E. Myers, 457–79. New York: Library of America. (Orig. pub. 1896.)

Keltner, Dacher. 2008. "In Defense of Teasing." *New York Times Magazine* (December 7), MM52-5.

———. 2009. *Born to Be Good: The Science of a Meaningful Life*. New York: W. W. Norton & Co.

Kindlon, Dan, and Michael Thompson. 1999/2000. *Raising Cain: Protecting the Emotional Lives of Boys*. New York: Ballantine Books.

Kristeva, Julia. 1991. *Strangers to Ourselves*. Translated by Leon S. Roudiez. New York: Columbia University Press.

Lartey, Emmanuel Y. 2003. *In Living Color: An Intercultural Approach to Pastoral Care and Counseling*, 2nd. ed. New York: Jessica Kingsley.

Le Goff, Jacques. 1984. *The Birth of Purgatory*. Translated by Arthur Goldhammer. Chicago: University of Chicago Press.

Leupold-Löwenthal, Harold. 1987. "Notes on Sigmund Freud's 'Analysis Terminable and Interminable.'" In *On Freud's 'Analysis Terminable and Interminable'*, ed. Joseph Sandler, 47–72. International Psychoanalytic Association Monograph No. 1.

Lynch, William F. 1965. *Images of Hope: Imagination as Healer of the Hopeless*. New York: The New American Library.

Martin, Dale B. 1999. *The Corinthian Body*. New Haven, CT: Yale University Press.

Marty, Martin E. 2009. "A Theological Dictionary: F Is for Friendship." *Christian Century* (February 24), 10.

Meilander, Gilbert. 1981. *Friendship: A Study in Theological Ethics*. Notre Dame, IN: University of Notre Dame Press.

Mitchell, David. 2006. *Black Swan Green*. New York: Random House.

Newman, John Henry Cardinal. 1888. *Verses on Various Occasions.* London: Longmans, Green & Co.

Nolan, Hamilton. 2008. "Does Nike Hate Gays? Or Do Gays Hate Basketball?" *www .Gawker.com.* (July 22). http://gawker.com/5027779/does-nike-hate-gays-or -do-gays-hate-basketball. Retrieved July 28, 2008.

Nygren, Anders. 1953. *Agape and Eros.* Translated by Philip L. Watson. Philadelphia: Westminster Press.

Phillips, Adam. 1995. *Terrors and Experts.* Cambridge, MA: Harvard University Press.

———. 2002. *Equals.* New York: Basic Books.

———. 2005. *Going Sane: Maps of Happiness.* New York: Fourth Estate/HarperCollins.

Phillips, Jock. 1987. *A Man's Country? The Image of the Pakeha Male—A History.* Auckland: Penguin Books.

Pollack, William S. 1998. *Real Boys: Rescuing Our Sons from the Myths of Boyhood.* New York: Ballantine Books.

Pollack, William S., with Todd Schuster. 2000. *Real Boys' Voices.* New York: Penguin Books.

Pruyser, Paul W. 1991. "Psychological Roots and Branches of Belief." In *Religion in Psychodynamic Perspective: The Contributions of Paul W. Pruyser,* ed. H. Newton Malony and Bernard Spilka, 155–69. New York: Oxford University Press. (Orig. pub. *Pastoral Psychology* 28 (1979): 8–20.)

Rogers, Carl R. 1961. *On Becoming a Person: A Therapist's View of Psychotherapy.* Boston: Houghton Mifflin.

Sandage, Scott A. 2005. *Born Losers: A History of Failure in America.* Cambridge, MA: Harvard University Press.

Sandler, Joseph, ed. 1987. *On Freud's "Analysis Terminable and Interminable."* International Psychoanalytic Monograph No. 1.

Saval, Malina. 2009. *The Secret Lives of Boys: Inside the Raw Emotional World of Male Teens.* New York: Basic Books.

Schweitzer, Carol L. Schnabl. 2008. "Gossip: The Grace Notes of Congregational Life." In *From Midterms to Ministry: Practical Theologians on Pastoral Beginnings,* ed. Allan Hugh Cole Jr., 191–203. Grand Rapids: Wm. B. Eerdmans Publishing Co.

Sedgwick, Eve Kosofsky. 1985. *Between Men: English Literature and Male Homosocial Desire.* New York: Columbia University Press.

Steinberg, Leo. 1983/1996. *The Sexuality of Christ in Renaissance Art and Modern Oblivion.* Chicago: University of Chicago Press.

Sullivan, Harry Stack. 1953/1997. *The Interpersonal Theory of Psychiatry.* Repr. New York: W. W. Norton & Co.

Vecchione, Patrice, ed. 2007. *Faith and Doubt: An Anthology of Poems.* New York: Henry Holt.

Vineberg, Steve. 2002. "Coming of Age." Review of the film *Y Tu Mamá También. Christian Century* (May 8), 37.

Warner, Judith. 2009. "Dude, You've Got Problems." *New York Times,* April 16, 2009, http://opinionater.blogs.nytimes.com/2009/04/16/who-are-you-calling -gay/?scp=1&sq=dude,%20you've%20got%20problems&st=cse.

Way, Niobe, and Judy Y. Chu, eds. 2004. *Adolescent Boys: Exploring Diverse Cultures of Boyhood.* New York: New York University Press.

Wexler, David B. 2009. *Men in Therapy: New Approaches for Effective Treatment.* New York: W. W. Norton & Co.

Wloszcyna, Susan. 2009. "Apatow Takes on Life and Death." *USA Today* (July 27), D1–2.

Worthen, Molly. 2009. "Who Would Jesus Smack Down?" *New York Times Magazine* (January 11), MM20.

Zimmerman, David and A. L. Bento Mostardiero. 1987. "On Teaching Freud's 'Analysis Terminable and Interminable.'" In *On Freud's "Analysis Terminable and Interminable,"* ed. Joseph Sandler, 89–109. International Psychoanalytical Association Monograph No. 1.

# Index

115